D1554187

K

Eli Coleman
S. Margretta Dwyer
Nathaniel J. Pallone
Editors

Sex Offender Treatment: Biological Dysfunction, Intrapsychic Conflict, Interpersonal Violence

*Pre-publication
REVIEWS,
COMMENTARIES,
EVALUATIONS . . .*

Sex Offender Treatment: Biological Dysfunction, Intrapsychic Conflict, Interpersonal Violence is a welcomed addition to the sex offender assessment and treatment literature. This well edited book contributes significant material to the field. *Sex Offender Treatment* offers a review of current assessment and treatment theory while addressing critical issues such as standards of care, use of phallometry, and working with specialized populations such as exhibitionists and developmentally disabled clients.

This resource also includes a very important chapter that addresses why some sex offenders fail at treatment and what might be done to work with clients who have learning disabilities. This book will make a valuable addition to the reader's professional library.

Robert E. Freeman-Longo, MRC, LPC
Director, The Safer Society Press

The Haworth Press, Inc.

SEX OFFENDER TREATMENT

Biological Dysfunction, Intrapsychic Conflict, Interpersonal Violence

SEX OFFENDER TREATMENT

Biological Dysfunction, Intrapsychic Conflict, Interpersonal Violence

ELI COLEMAN

S. MARGRETTA DWYER

NATHANIEL J. PALLONE
Editors

THE HAWORTH PRESS, INC.
New York • London

Sex Offender Treatment: Biological Dysfunction, Intrapsychic Conflict, Interpersonal Violence has also been published as *Journal of Offender Rehabilitation*, Volume 23, Numbers 3/4 1996.

The development, preparation, and publication of this work has been undertaken with great care. However, the publisher, employees, editors, and agents of The Haworth Press and all imprints of The Haworth Press, Inc., including The Haworth Medical Press and Pharmaceutical Products Press, are not responsible for any errors contained herein or for consequences that may ensue from use of materials or information contained in this work. Opinions expressed by the author(s) are not necessarily those of The Haworth Press, Inc.

The Haworth Press, Inc., 10 Alice Street, Binghamton, NY 13904-1580 USA

Library of Congress Cataloging-in-Publication Data

Sex offender treatment : biological dysfunction, intrapsychic conflict, interpersonal violence / Eli Coleman, S. Margretta Dwyer, Nathaniel J. Pallone, editors.
    p. cm.
    Includes bibliographical references.
    ISBN 1-56024-834-3 (alk. paper)
    1. Sex offenders–Rehabilitation. 2. Sex offenders–Psychology. I. Coleman, Eli. II. Dwyer, S. Margretta. III. Pallone, Nathaniel J.
RC560.S47S466 1996
616.85'8306–dc20   96-20107
                                           CIP

INDEXING & ABSTRACTING

Contributions to this publication are selectively indexed or abstracted in print, electronic, online, or CD-ROM version(s) of the reference tools and information services listed below. This list is current as of the copyright date of this publication. See the end of this section for additional notes.

- *Abstracts of Research in Pastoral Care & Counseling,* Loyola College, 7135 Minstrel Way, Suite 101, Columbia, MD 21045

- *Cambridge Scientific Abstracts, Risk Abstracts,* Environmental Routenet (accessed via INTERNET), 7200 Wisconsin Avenue #601, Bethesda, MD 20814

- *CNPIEC Reference Guide: Chinese National Directory of Foreign Periodicals,* P.O. Box 88, Beijing, People's Republic of China

- *Criminal Justice Periodical Index,* University Microfilms, Inc., 300 North Zeeb Road, Ann Arbor, MI 48106

- *Criminal Justice Abstracts,* Willow Tree Press, 15 Washington Street, 4th Floor, Newark, NJ 07102

- *Criminology, Penology and Police Science Abstracts,* Kugler Publications, P. O. Box 11188, 1001 GD Amsterdam, The Netherlands

- *ERIC Clearinghouse on Counseling and Student Services (ERIC/CASS),* University of North Carolina-Greensboro, 101 Park Building, Greensboro, NC 27412-5001

- *Family Studies Database (online and CD-ROM)*, Peters Technology Transfer, 306 East Baltimore Pike, 2nd Floor, Media, PA 19063

- *Family Violence & Sexual Assault Bulletin,* Family Violence & Sexual Assault Institute, 1310 Clinic Drive, Tyler, TX 75701

(continued)

- *IBZ International Bibliography of Periodical Literature,* Zeller Verlag GmbH & Co., P.O.B. 1949, d-49009 Osnabruck, Germany

- *Index to Periodical Articles Related to Law,* University of Texas, 727 East 26th Street, Austin, TX 78705

- *INTERNET ACCESS (& additional networks) Bulletin Board for Libraries ("BUBL"), coverage of information resources on INTERNET, JANET, and other networks.*
  - JANET X.29: UK.AC.BATH.BUBL or 00006012101300
  - TELNET: BUBL.BATH.AC.UK or 138.38.32.45 login 'bubl'
  - Gopher: BUBL.BATH.AC.UK (138.32.32.45). Port 7070
  - World Wide Web: http: / / www.bubl.bath.ac.uk./BUBL/ home.html
  - NISSWAIS: telnetniss.ac.uk (for the NISS gateway)
  The Andersonian Library, Curran Building, 101 St. James Road, Glasgow G4 ONS, Scotland

- *Mental Health Abstracts (online through DIALOG),* IFI/Plenum Data Company, 3202 Kirkwood Highway, Wilmington, DE 19808

- *National Criminal Justice Reference Service,* National Institute of Justice/NCJRS, Mail Stop 2L/1600 Research Boulevard, Rockville, MD 20850

- *NIAAA Alcohol and Alcohol Problems Science Database (ETOH),* National Institute on Alcohol Abuse and Alcoholism, 1400 Eye Street NW, Suite 600, Washington, DC 20005

- *PASCAL International Bibliography T205: Sciences de l'information Documentation,* INIST/CNRS-Service Gestion des Documents Primaires, 2, allee du Parc de Brabois, F-54514 Vandoeuvre-les-Nancy, Cedex, France

- *Referativnyi Zhurnal (Abstracts Journal of the Institute of Scientific Information of the Republic of Russia),* The Institute of Scientific Information, Baltijskaja ul., 14, Moscow, A-219, Republic of Russia

- *Sage Urban Studies Abstracts (SUSA),* Sage Publications, Inc., 2455 Teller Road, Newbury Park, CA 91320

(continued)

- *Social Planning/Policy & Development Abstracts (SOPODA)*, Sociological Abstracts, Inc., P. O. Box 22206, San Diego, CA 92192-0206

- *Social Work Abstracts*, National Association of Social Workers, 750 First Street NW, 8th Floor, Washington, DC 20002

- *Sociological Abstracts (SA)*, Sociological Abstracts, Inc., P. O. Box 22206, San Diego, CA 92192-0206

- *Special Educational Needs Abstracts*, Carfax Information Systems, P. O. Box 25, Abingdon, Oxfordshire OX14 3UE, United Kingdom

- *Violence and Abuse Abstracts: A Review of Current Literature on Interpersonal Violence (VAA)*, Sage Publications, Inc., 2455 Teller Road, Newbury Park, CA 91320

SPECIAL BIBLIOGRAPHIC NOTES

*related to special journal issues (separates)
and indexing/abstracting*

☐ indexing/abstracting services in this list will also cover material in any "separate" that is co-published simultaneously with Haworth's special thematic journal issue or DocuSerial. Indexing/abstracting usually covers material at the article/chapter level.

☐ monographic co-editions are intended for either non-subscribers or libraries which intend to purchase a second copy for their circulating collections.

☐ monographic co-editions are reported to all jobbers/wholesalers/approval plans. The source journal is listed as the "series" to assist the prevention of duplicate purchasing in the same manner utilized for books-in-series.

☐ to facilitate user/access services all indexing/abstracting services are encouraged to utilize the co-indexing entry note indicated at the bottom of the first page of each article/chapter/contribution.

☐ this is intended to assist a library user of any reference tool (whether print, electronic, online, or CD-ROM) to locate the monographic version if the library has purchased this version but not a subscription to the source journal.

☐ individual articles/chapters in any Haworth publication are also available through the Haworth Document Delivery Services (HDDS).

SEX OFFENDER TREATMENT

Biological Dysfunction, Intrapsychic Conflict, Interpersonal Violence

CONTENTS

SEX OFFENDER TREATMENT
Biological Dysfunction, Intrapsychic Conflict, Interpersonal Violence. Pp. 1-3.

Introduction and Dedication

ELI COLEMAN
University of Minnesota

S. MARGRETTA DWYER
University of Minnesota

Since 1989, we have co-chaired the three international conferences in Minneapolis, Minnesota, on the treatment of sex offenders. These conferences were sponsored by the Program in Human Sexuality, Department of Family Practice and Community Health of the School of Medicine at the University of Minnesota, Minneapolis, Minnesota, USA. After the second conference in 1991, we published a selection of papers from that conference in a special issue of the *Journal of Offender Rehabilitation* which was also issued in book form under the title *Sex Offender Treatment: Psychological and Medical Approaches*. The present volume contains a selection of papers from the Third International Congress on the Treatment of Sex Offenders held in September 1994.

The Fourth International Congress will be held in Amsterdam in September 1995 and will be chaired by Lex van Naerssan, Ph.D., professor of psychology at Utrecht University in The Netherlands, and co-sponsored by the Program in Human Sexuality, School of Medicine, University of Minnesota. We believe sponsoring these conferences has been a successful way to bring professionals together to present their research and treatment models. The participants in these conferences have enjoyed the intellectual stimulation to advance their own thinking and improve their research and treatment methodologies.

The international nature of the conference has helped us reflect on our concepts and constructs by examining them from a cross-cultural viewpoint. We continue to recognize that what is considered offensive in one country is not necessarily so in another country. Laws are time- and culture-dependent. How we treat sex offenders in different parts of the world differs greatly. Ultimately, however, we are trying to improve the effectiveness of treatment of sex offenders throughout the world. We hope this volume informs the reader of the most recent research in this area as well as spurs interest into scientific achievements in the future.

This second volume begins with an updated/revised version of the standards of care for the treatment of adult sex offenders. A committee was formed after the Second Conference to make changes in the proposed standards that we first published in 1990. The committee was composed of scholars in the field from the United States, Canada, Germany, and Austria. The committee members made excellent recommendations for changes and these were incorporated into the current publication. This revised version was approved by the participants in the Third International Congress on the Treatment of Sex Offenders. The Standards will be an on-going development project and reviewed at future International Conferences, with input from scientists around the world. We invite your comments and suggestions as to revisions. We hope these standards will serve their purpose in providing a guide to increasing the effectiveness of treatment of sex offenders. The Standards of Care are also helpful in analyzing new data and giving the reader a basic understanding of sex offender treatment as it stands today, so it seems appropriate to begin this second volume with this paper.

Other articles in this volume probe into the nature of interpersonal violence and aggression and further understanding of pedophilia and exhibitionism. Still others address the importance of good assessment techniques, issues affecting victims and families of sex offenders, why treatment does not work for some sex offenders, medical problems associated with sex offenders, and working with special populations of sex offenders, especially those with learning difficulties or mental retardation.

Each of the authors in this volume has devoted many years of his or her career to this field. They come from varied backgrounds and these differences are reflected in the ways the articles are written. All authors recognize past knowledge, present new information, and look to the future for further understanding. We hope these papers will challenge the reader into conducting more research that will help scientists and practitioners more fully understand the phenomenon of sex offending and improve our treatment approaches.

DEDICATION

We dedicate this volume to the two persons who were honored and received awards for their outstanding contributions to the field of sex offender treatment at the Third International Congress of Sex Offenders.

Ingo Wiederholt, Med. Dr.

Dr. Wiederholt, a psychiatrist from Munich, Germany, was recognized for his life-long contributions in the treatment of sex offenders. He has always had a great devotion to his patients. Because of illness, Ingo was unable to attend the conference; however, he sent a letter to the attendees giving his thanks and telling them that he felt great satisfaction for his many years of treating individuals who had committed sex offenses.

Judith Becker, Ph.D.

Dr. Becker, a psychologist and a professor of psychiatry and psychology at the University of Arizona, USA. was recognized for her highly significant contributions in the area of research and treatment of juvenile sex offenders. By studying and treating adolescent sex offenders, Judith's work has provided us with very valuable information as we look to the future of abuse prevention.

SEX OFFENDER TREATMENT
Biological Dysfunction, Intrapsychic Conflict, Interpersonal Violence. Pp. 5-11.

Standards of Care for the Treatment of Adult Sex Offenders

ELI COLEMAN
S. MARGRETTA DWYER
GENE ABEL, M.D.
WOLFGANG BERNER, M.D.
JAMES BREILING
JAN HINDMAN
FAY HONEY KNOPP
RON LANGEVIN
FRIEDEMANN PFAFFLIN, M.D.

ABSTRACT A proposed version of these standards was first produced and published in the *Journal of Offender Rehabilitation* through input from a variety of professionals and from professional meetings (Coleman and Dwyer, 1990). Since that time, the present writers (along with Kurt Freund, M.D., William Marshall, Ph.D., and William Murphy, Ph.D.) have reviewed those proposed standards and have made the changes incorporated into this version. The Standards of Care herein were unanimously endorsed by voice vote by the participants in the Third International Congress on the Treatment of Sex Offenders held in Minneapolis, Minnesota, on September 20-22, 1994. The authors invite feedback from readers. Further revisions are anticipated and will be reviewed by current committee members and at future International Congresses on the Treatment of Sex Offenders. Please address comments to Eli Coleman, Ph.D., Director and Associate Professor, Program in Human Sexuality, School of Medicine, University of Minnesota, 1300 S. 2nd Street, Suite 180, Minneapolis, MN 55454 USA. *[Copies of this paper are available from The Haworth Document Delivery Service: 1-800-342-9678.]*

From puberty through adulthood, males more than females experience erotic fantasies and dreams of a paraphilic type. A paraphilia is a condition of compulsive response to, or dependence upon, an unusual and unacceptable stimulus in the imagery of fantasy, for optimal initiation and fantasy during solo masturbation or intercourse with a partner.

There are well over 40 types of paraphilias which have been identified and defined (Money, 1986). Only eight of them are listed in the *Diagnostic and Statistical Manual of Mental Disorders* (American Psychiatric Association, 1987), where the remainder are subsumed under, "not otherwise specified." Given the socio-cultural-religious-political climate, some paraphilias are legally considered to be sex crimes which are punishable by law. In legal codes, crimes against nature and affronts to socially acceptable sexual behavior are criminalized and are regarded as sex offenses. These crimes have included statutory rape, violent rape, child molesting, exhibitionism, voyeurism and incest. What is considered a sexual crime and the standards of punishment are state, time, and culture dependent. Over time, there have been many revisions of the criminal sexual codes (Pallone, 1990).

For the most part, today sex offenders may be fined, ordered to psychological or medical treatment, and/or imprisoned. For first-time offenders, and for lesser offenses, there is a greater likelihood of probation, subject to some professional sex offender treatment.

Although treatment is costly and unaffordable by some, not to treat can be more costly emotionally and psychologically for the offender, for the victims and future victims, and for society.

Today there is more scientific evidence and consensus among professionals that paraphilias are psychosexual disorders. By contrast, the predominant view of the lay public around the world is that sex crimes can be eradicated with punishment and/or death. This predominant view is not supported by scientific evidence, and the scientific community needs to continue to promote awareness that sex crimes can also be the manifestations of biomedical/psychiatric/psychological illnesses for which people must be treated, rather than simply punished.

In recent decades, the demand for sex offender treatment has increased, as have the number and variety of possible biomedical/ psychiatric/psychological treatments. The rationale upon which such treatments have been offered has become more and more complex. Various "appropriate care" philosophies have been suggested by many professionals who have identified themselves as experts on the topic of sex offenders.

In an effort to establish minimal acceptable guidelines for the treatment of sex offenders, the authors present the following Standards of Care as guidelines which might be helpful to enhance the ethical and professional treatment of sex offenders throughout the world.

STATEMENT OF PURPOSE

Although each profession has its own standards of care, the following are minimal recommendations of Standards of Care. It is recommended that professionals involved in the treatment of sex offenders use the following *minimal criteria* for the evaluation of their work. It is recommended that the reasons for exceptions to these standards, in the management of any individual case, be very carefully documented.

DEFINITIONS

Standards of Care

Standards of Care are exactly what is implied: standards for caring for patients. In this case: care and treatment of sex offenders.

Paraphilia

Paraphilia is an erotosexual condition occurring in men and women who are responsive to, or dependent upon, an unusual or socially unacceptable stimulus in the imagery or fantasy for optimal initiation and maintenance of erotic-sexual arousal and the facilitation or attainment of orgasm.

Sex Offense

If paraphilia is enacted in actual behavior rather than in erotic fantasy or dream, it may qualify as a criminal sex offense. There is great discrepancy throughout the world as to what constitutes a sex offense (Pallone, 1990).

Sex Offender

An individual who commits a sexual crime as legally defined in his or her own culture or legal jurisdiction.

Psychological Treatment

Psychological treatment refers to the array of therapies which have been designed to treat sex offenders. Different treatments are based on different psychological and psychiatric theories regarding the origin of the paraphilic sex offending, for example, psychoanalytic, cognitive, behavioral, social learning, and family systems theories. Psychological or psychiatric care can be provided in individual, couple, family or group settings. The purpose of treatment is an attempt to prevent further offending behavior and further victimization of others.

Biomedical Treatment

Biomedical treatment refers to the use of pharmacological treatment or neurosurgery for the purpose of altering sexual fantasies, impulses, and behavior. Pharmacologic therapy has included (but is not limited to) the use of antiandrogens, antidepressants, and antianxiety, antiepileptic, antipsychotic, or other medications.

Surgical treatment might involve brain surgery to correct temporal lobe seizures. With the advent of effective chemotherapies which alter the erotosexual response, the necessity of psychosurgery in the absence of epileptic foci has been rendered inappropriate.

PROFESSIONAL COMPETENCE

Possession of an academic degree in a behavioral science, medicine, or for the provision of psychosocial clinical services does not necessarily attest to the possession of sufficient competence to conduct assessment or treatment of paraphilic or sex offending problems. Persons assessing and/or treating sex offenders should have clinical training and experience in the diagnosis and treatment of a range of psychiatric and psychological conditions and also specialized training and experience in the assessment and treatment of paraphilic and sex offender problems. This would generally be reflected by appropriate licensure as a psychiatrist, psychologist, or clinical therapist and by documentation of training and experience in the diagnosis and treatment of a broad range of sexual conditions, including paraphilic disorders and sex offenses. Treatment providers must be competent in making a differential diagnosis. The following *minimal standards* for a professional should be adhered to:

☐ 1. A minimum of a master's degree or its equivalent or medical degree in a clinical field granted by an institution of education accredited by a national/regional accrediting board.

☐ 2. Demonstrated competence in therapy as indicated by a license (or its equivalent from a certifying body) to practice medicine, psychology, clinical social work, professional counseling, or marriage and family counseling.

☐ 3. Demonstrated specialized competence in counseling and diagnosis of sexual disorders and sex offending behaviors as documentable by training or supervised clinical experience, along with continuing education.

ANTECEDENTS TO SEX OFFENDER TREATMENT

☐ 1. Prospective patients should receive an extensive evaluation of their sex offending behavior which would include appropriateness for treatment, amenability for treatment, psychological/psychiatric diagnoses, evaluation for safety and protection for the community.

☐ 2. A thorough physical examination is recommended especially when physical problems are suspected that might require specific treatment, i.e., heart problems, high blood pressure, liver damage, brain lesions, and epilepsy.

☐ 3. Prospective patients should receive a psychological and/or psychiatric examination which would rule out other psychological/psychiatric disorders. If any other psychological/psychiatric disorders are found, treatment of such disorder requires separate [appropriate] treatment prior to treatment for paraphilic or sex offending behavior.

☐ 4. If medication is deemed necessary or requested by the patient, the patient must be given information regarding the benefits and potential side effects or disadvantages of biomedical treatment.

THE PRINCIPLES OF STANDARDS OF CARE

☐ *Principle 1:* While treatment effectiveness of adult sex offenders has not been clearly demonstrated, there are indications that some kinds of treatment may be effective in managing and reducing recidivism with some types of sex offenders.

☐ *Principle 2:* Sex offender treatment is viewed by offenders as an elective process (the choice is theirs), since individuals may not view their sex offending behavior as psychologically or medically pathological.

☐ *Principle 3:* The evaluation of treatment of sex offenders requires specialized skills not usually associated with the professional training of clinical therapists or medical professionals.

☐ *Principle 4:* Sex offender treatment is performed for the purpose of improving quality of life and is considered a humane treatment for people who have committed a sex offense and to prevent the patient from engaging in further sex offending behavior.

☐ *Principle 5:* The patient with a documented biomedical abnormality is first treated by procedures commonly accepted as appropriate for any such medical conditions before beginning, or in conjunction with, psychotherapy.

☐ *Principle 6:* The patient having a psychiatric diagnosis (i.e., schizophrenia) is first treated by procedures commonly accepted as appropriate for the psychiatric diagnoses, or, if appropriate, for both simultaneously.

☐ *Principle 7:* Sex offender treatment may involve a variety of therapeutic approaches. It is important for professionals to keep abreast of this growing and developing field and provide the most efficacious treatments which have been demonstrated through outcome studies. Some of the most effective approaches available today involve cognitive and behavioral therapies which include increase in victim empathy, control over offending urges and relapse prevention.

☐ *Principle 8:* A treatment plan may involve the use of pharmacotherapy which typically relieves some sexual arousal and fantasy. Impulse control is thereby increased and individuals feel less driven by their sexual compulsion or their paraphilic fantasy imagery.

☐ *Principle 9:* The current treatment of sex offenders often causes special legal problems for the professionals offering such care and treatment. Therefore, the professional should work with the criminal justice system in a professional and cooperative manner.

☐ *Principle 10:* Sex offenders often have a need for a follow-up treatment/visits, and this should be encouraged or possibly required.

☐ *Principle 11:* It is unethical to charge patients for services which are essentially for research and which do not directly benefit the patient.

☐ *Principle 12:* In order to effectively persuade the professionals in the legal community as well as society in general about the efficacy of sex offender treatment, professionals should cooperate with and carry out scientifically sound treatment outcome research.

☐ *Principle 13:* Sex offenders often must face legal proceedings, and professionals treating these individuals must be prepared to appear in court if necessary.

☐ *Principle 14:* Sex offenders are given the same rights to medical and psychological privacies as any other patient group, with the exception of where the law requires otherwise, i.e., reporting laws, subpoenaing of records.

REFERENCES

American Psychiatric Association. (1987). *Diagnostic and Statistical Manual of the American Psychiatric Association (DSM-III-R)*. Washington, D.C.: American Psychiatric Association.

Coleman, E. and Dwyer, S. M. (1990). Proposed standards of care for the treatment of adult sex offenders. *Journal of Offender Rehabilitation,* 16(1/2), 93-106.

Money, J. (1986). *Lovemaps: Clinical Concepts of Sexual/Erotic Health & Pathology, Paraphilia, and Gender Transposition in Childhood, Adolescence & Maturity.* Buffalo: Prometheus.

Pallone, N. J. (1990). *Rehabilitating Criminal Sexual Psychopaths: Legislative Mandates, Clinical Quandaries.* New Brunswick, NJ: Transaction Books.

AUTHORS' NOTES

Address correspondence to Dr. Eli Coleman, Program in Human Sexuality, School of Medicine, University of Minnesota, 1300 S. 2nd Street, Suite 180, Minneapolis, MN 55454 USA.

SEX OFFENDER TREATMENT
Biological Dysfunction, Intrapsychic Conflict, Interpersonal Violence. Pp. 13-37.

The Confluence Model of Sexual Aggression: Combining Hostile Masculinity and Impersonal Sex

NEIL M. MALAMUTH
University of California, Los Angeles

CHRISTOPHER L. HEAVEY
University of Nevada, Las Vegas

DANIEL LINZ
University of California, Santa Barbara

ABSTRACT A model of the characteristics of sexually aggressive men is described which emphasizes the convergence of several interrelated factors. After enumerating the major factors included in the model and the way we have assessed each, we present data showing that these factors form two largely independent constellations, labeled *hostile masculinity* and *impersonal sexual orientation*. The development of the model is considered in the context of theory and research emphasizing the role of sexual and/or power motives underlying rape and other forms of sexual aggression. We compare some aspects of our model to the influential work of Donald Mosher and his associates in assessing the links between a "macho personality" and sexual aggression. Finally, we describe a "risk" analysis which illustrates the potential relevance of our model to clinical prediction. *[Copies of this paper are available from The Haworth Document Delivery Service: 1-800-342-9678.]*

Common wisdom and psychological research on rape and other forms of sexual aggression may be characterized by three views concerning the underlying motives for such behavior. The first emphasizes sexual motives whereas the second argues that power motives and desire for control are primary. The third view suggests that rape is a product or a synthesis of both of these types of motives.

Rape as Sex

As Palmer (1988) notes, until the early 1970's researchers held the view that while many motivations could be involved in any given rape, sex was the dominant motive (Amir, 1971; Gebhard et al., 1965; LeVine, 1959). For example, Kanin (1977, 1984) concluded that sexual aggression among college students is a function of placing a relatively high emphasis on the acquisition of sex experiences with the *incidental* use of force, "as a means to an end," to obtain sexual gratifications. The predominant underlying motivation for rape is assumed to be sexual rather than asserting power over women or a desire to hurt women. In this view, sexual aggression is seen as a form of temporary "sexual acting out."

Manifestations of sexual aggression in early adulthood are not thought to be indicative of problematic social interactions with women later in life. Sexual aggression, once it has occurred, is expected to decline with age both as sex drive dissipates and the availability of a steady sexual partner increases. Criticisms of this approach take issue with the postulation of a sex drive per se that declines with age as a primary motive for sexual aggression. In fact, the belief that rape will only occur among men who are sexually deprived is not substantiated by empirical research. For example, most rapists have stable sexual partners (Sanford & Fetter, 1979). Although such data do not directly contradict some theories incorporating sexual motives, they do cast doubt on some simplistic views of "rape as sex" (Palmer, 1988).

Rape as Power

The second position is that rape is nearly exclusively a matter of power, expressed by the use of violence, rather than sex. This view, attributed to the feminist movement by some authors (e.g., Sanders,

1980), sees the rapist as using sex to attain control and domination (Palmer, 1988). The implications here, unlike the sex only perspective, are that rape and sexual violence are expressions of a more generalized tendency toward dominance and control of women and that early tendencies toward domination may portend difficulties with women across the life span.

This view has also been criticized. Often, critics say, when proponents of this view maintain that rape is not a matter of "sex," they are referring to sexual motivations, moods, or drives associated with "honest courtship," love, and pair bonding. This definition of sex is unduly limiting (Palmer, 1988). Many men are capable of impersonal sex that is void of feelings of tenderness and affection. Most proponents of the power only perspective have not incorporated motivations or drives for impersonal sex.

Combining Motives

In the present article, we summarize some of the findings of a research program, studying men from the general population, which reveals that sexual aggressors are most likely to be relatively high on characteristics which we label as "hostile masculinity" and "impersonal sex." These correspond, to some degree, to power and to sexual motivations, respectively. Before describing that model in greater detail, it is important to recognize other researchers who have also taken the position that both sexual and control-related motivations contribute to sexual aggression (e.g., Clark & Lewis, 1977; Ellis, 1989; Finkelhor, 1986; Mosher & Sirkin, 1984; Thornhill & Thornhill, 1992).

Although a discussion of the similarities and differences between each of those positions and ours is beyond the scope of the present article, we would like to briefly describe the important work of Donald Mosher and his associates. While we do not suggest that there is any necessary incompatibility between our profile of aggressors and theirs, we would like to note some differences, since at first glance our model and theirs may appear quite similar. We hope that future research will result in a successful integration of both models.

Mosher and associates argue that the profile of the sexual aggressor is one who has a "macho" personality, reflecting "an exaggerated masculine style" (Mosher & Sirkin, 1984, p. 151). It includes calloused attitudes toward sex, a tendency to embrace violence and an attraction to dangerous experiences (Mosher & Sirkin, 1984). This personality profile is measured by the Hypermasculinity scale developed by these investigators. Mosher and Anderson (1986) examined the relationship between this scale and self-reported sexual aggression. There was an overall significant relationship between these two measures, r (173) = .33, p < .001. However, it appears that this association is largely due to the Calloused Sex Attitudes subscale, which was relatively highly correlated with sexual aggression, r (173) = .55. The other two subscales show significant, but considerably lower correlations with sexual aggression ranging from .23 to .26. Unfortunately, Mosher and Anderson (1986) do not report a regression analysis controlling for the overlap between the three subscales and enabling the determination of whether the latter two subscales added any significant prediction beyond that achieved by the Calloused Sex Attitudes subscale alone [Note 1].

We contend that a model of sexual aggression which incorporates several motives, factors or elements needs to demonstrate the superiority of the multiple-component model to a model focusing on single variables or motives only. The findings of Mosher and Anderson raise questions regarding whether they have actually identified several elements that contribute to sexual aggression or whether only one aspect of their model is actually directly relevant to sexually aggressive behavior. As we hope to demonstrate below, our findings suggest that each of the multiple components we have included in our model enables better prediction of sexual aggression than models that do not incorporate these components.

In addition, some key differences between our construct of "Hostile Masculinity" and Mosher's "Hypermasculinity" concern (1) the degree of specificity in the mechanisms hypothesized to cause aggression towards women, and (2) in the emphasis on hostility towards women. Mosher's work perceives aggression towards women as one manifestation of a general ". . . desire to appear powerful and to be dominant" (Mosher & Sirkin, 1984, 151). Mosher's work emphasizes general tendencies associated with violence, danger, and sensation seeking characteristics.

Although we also recognize that such characteristics can contribute to aggression against women and may be particularly useful within a hierarchical model that includes both general and specific mechanisms (Malamuth, 1988), we have placed more emphasis on specific mechanisms pertaining to men's attempts to control women's sexuality and other aspects of women's behavior (Malamuth, Heavey & Linz, 1993; Malamuth & Thornhill, 1994). We have also emphasized the role of men's hostility as a cause of aggression against women, which is not emphasized in Mosher's construct of the "macho" personality. Although we do not contend that the levels of sexual aggressors' hostility are outside the "normal" range, we suggest that this construct, as reflected in the Hostility Toward Women scale we developed (Check, 1985; Check, Malamuth, Elias, & Barton, 1985), plays an important role in this area.

THE CONFLUENCE MODEL OF SEXUAL AGGRESSION

Our model suggests that sexual aggression may be conceptualized as resulting from the *convergence* of several factors (Malamuth, 1986). Our approach is similar to some other theorizing, such as that of Sternberg and Lubart (1991) regarding creativity. These theorists have noted the utility of a multivariate approach in predicting creative performance. Their model includes intellectual processes, knowledge, intellectual style, personality, motivation, and environmental context as converging factors. Creative performance results from a *confluence* of these elements. Similarly, we maintain that sexual aggression is the result of the confluence or interactive combination of the motivation, disinhibition and opportunity predictor variables. A relatively high level on each of these characteristics contributes to sexual aggression, although we do not argue that any particular factor constitutes a necessary condition for such aggression to occur. We also suggest that the motivation and disinhibition factors form constellations that may be meaningfully organized into two major paths, so that sexual aggression may be best understood as the interaction between (1) relatively high levels of "impersonal" (sometimes referred to herein as "promiscuous") sex and (2) hostile, controlling characteristics which both enable an individual to overcome the inhibitions that could prevent the use of coercive tactics and enhance the gratification derived by a man using sex as a means of asserting power and venting anger.

Additionally, our model suggests that factors contributing to sexual aggression may be expressed in behaviors that are not *overtly* aggressive. In other words, sexually aggressive behavior is not considered an isolated response but an expression of a way of dealing with social relationships and conflicts with women in general. We have predicted that many of the same factors that contribute to self-reports of sexual aggression and aggression in the laboratory would also contribute to other forms of dysfunctional relationships with women, such as men's domineeringness in conversations with women (Malamuth & Briere, 1986; Malamuth & Thornhill, 1994) and a generally poor quality of romantic relationships.

Early research (Malamuth, 1986) related to this model concentrated on three interrelated categories of proximate causes of aggression against women: (1) the *motivation* to commit the aggressive act, (2) *reductions in inhibitions* that might prevent aggression from being carried out, and (3) the *opportunity* for aggressive acts to occur. While it is useful to think of these as distinct categories, in reality they may sometimes not be clearly separable. In our research program we have primarily used six predictor variables conceived as falling into these three categories. We should note, however, that while differentiating these factors into the three categories is theoretically useful (Malamuth, 1986), some of these six variables may have effects at multiple category levels.

Measurement of Variables in Confluence Model

(1) Sexual Responsiveness to Rape

The ratio of sexual arousal to rape portrayals compared with arousal to consenting sex portrayals has been suggested as a discriminator between rapists and nonrapists (Abel, Barlow, Blanchard & Guild, 1977; Barbaree & Marshall, 1991; Quinsey, 1984). Although considerable research has shown that sexual responsiveness to rape alone is not a particularly good indicator of being a rapist (e.g., Malamuth & Check, 1981), such responsiveness may reveal some motivation to sexually aggress. We have used direct genital measurement of physiological arousal (i.e., penile tumescence) to depictions of rape as compared with arousal to mutually consenting sex.

(2) Dominance Motive

The view has been widely expressed that the desire to dominate women is an important motive of sexual aggression (e.g., Brownmiller, 1975). Studies of convicted rapists have shown the importance of the offender's desire to conquer and sexually dominate his victim (e.g., Groth, 1979; Scully & Marolla, 1985). The self-report measure used in our research to assess this dominance construct was part of a larger instrument developed by Nelson (1979) that asked respondents the degree to which various feelings and sensations are important to them as motives for sexual behavior. The subscale assessing dominance (8 items) refers to the degree to which feelings of control over one's partner motivate sexuality (e.g., "I enjoy the feeling of having someone in my grasp"; "I enjoy the conquest").

(3) Hostility Toward Women

Studies of convicted rapists have also emphasized the role of hostility toward women (e.g., Groth, 1979). Such hostility may motivate the behavior as well as remove inhibitions when the victim shows signs of suffering (Malamuth, 1986). This construct was measured by the Hostility Toward Women scale (30 items) mentioned earlier (Check, 1985; Check, Malamuth, Elias & Barton, 1985).

Examples of items are "Women irritate me a great deal more than they are aware of," and "When I look back at what's happened to me, I don't feel at all resentful towards the women in my life."

(4) Attitudes Facilitating Aggression Against Women

Burt (1978, 1980) theorized that certain attitudes play an important role in contributing to sexual aggression by acting as "psychological releasers or neutralizers, allowing potential rapists to turn off social prohibitions against injuring or using others" (1978, 282). She developed several scales to measure attitudes that directly and indirectly support aggression against women. The scale developed by Burt that we have used most frequently (because it measures attitudes that directly condone the use of force in sexual relationships) has been the Acceptance of Interpersonal Violence (AIV) against women scale.

Five of the six items measure attitudes supporting violence against women, whereas the sixth concerns revenge. An example of an item is "Sometimes the only way a man can get a cold woman turned on is to use force." In some of the studies we have also used two of Burt's other scales, those assessing Rape Myth Acceptance (RMA) and Adversarial Sexual Beliefs. These scales assess attitudes more indirectly supportive of aggression.

(5) Antisocial Personality Characteristics/Psychoticism

Rapaport and Burkhart (1984) suggested that, although certain factors may provide a context for sexually aggressive behavior, the actual expression of such aggression occurs only if the person also has certain personality "deficits." Studies assessing such deficits (e.g., psychopathy) have generally failed to show correlations between such measures alone and sexual aggression (e.g., Koss & Leonard, 1984) although such measures do relate to antisocial behavior generally. Moreover, testing of Rapaport and Burkhart's proposal requires assessment of the interaction between general antisocial personality characteristics and specific factors related to aggression against women. In our research, we have sometimes measured such general antisocial personality characteristics with the Psychoticism (P) scale of the Eysenck Personality Questionnaire (Eysenck, 1978).

(6) Sexual Experience

The Sexual Behavior Inventory (Bentler, 1968) was used to assess subjects' conventional heterosexual experiences including such acts as fondling of breasts, intercourse and oral sex. In some of the research, we also assessed other aspects of sexual experience, such as age of first intercourse, the number of people with whom the subject has had intercourse, and extra-relationship sex.

In some of our research (e.g., Malamuth, 1986), sexual experience was primarily treated as an "opportunity" variable, reasoning that the degree to which men engaged in dating and sexual behavior may affect the extent to which they had the opportunity to use coercive tactics. In later research (e.g., Malamuth et al., 1991) we placed more emphasis on this variable as an individual differences characteristic of men. In general, our research to date has been primarily focused on men's traits and has not given much attention to how such characteristics may interact with situational variables, such as the opportunity dimension. As the research progresses further, it clearly will be important to give greater attention to such situational factors.

Dependent Variable: Sexual Aggression

Sexual aggression, our primary dependent variable, was measured by the self-report instrument developed by Koss and Oros (1982). It assesses a continuum of sexual aggression including psychological pressure, physical coercion, attempted rape and rape. Subjects respond using a true-false format to nine descriptions of different levels of sexual coercion. An example of an item is "I have had sexual intercourse with a woman when she didn't want to because I used some degree of physical force (twisting her arm, holding her down, etc.)." Although sexual aggression generally was used as the dependent measure we were interested in predicting, we have also used sexual aggression as a predictor of other forms of conflict in relationships with women in our longitudinal study.

Early Tests of Multiple Factors in the Model

Malamuth (1986) began to explore this model by testing the association of the six predictor variables discussed above to sexual aggression. These predictors included arousal to sexual aggression, dominance as a motive for sex, hostility toward women, attitudes supporting violence, psychoticism and sexual experience. Data were available for 95 subjects on all of these predictors and for 155 on all of the measures except sexual arousal (sixty subjects did not wish to participate in this type of assessment).

To begin, the simple correlation of each of these predictors with sexual aggression was examined. All of the predictors except psychoticism were significantly related to self-reported sexual aggression. The association between psychoticism and sexual aggression only approached significance. Interestingly, the one measure which did not share method variance with sexual aggression, the penile tumescence index of sexual arousal, showed relatively strong relationship with aggression (at $r = .43$, $p < .001$).

Next, Malamuth (1986) examined whether these predictors provided overlapping prediction of sexual aggression. When all of the six predictors were entered into a regression equation, four made significant unique contributions (arousal to sexual aggression, Hostility Toward Women, attitudes supporting violence and sexual experience). Thus, these predictors did not provide predominantly overlapping prediction in that a combination of them was superior to any individual one for predicting levels of sexual aggressiveness.

Finally, Malamuth (1986) examined whether a model containing interactive terms would afford greater prediction than that of a simple additive model. Comparison revealed that models containing interactive effects accounted for a significantly greater percentage of the variance (45% for all 155 subjects and 75% for the 95 subjects) than equations containing additive effects only (30% and 45%, respectively).

To further examine the interactive nature of the predictors and to illustrate the potential for clinical prediction, each subject was classified as having either a high or low score on each predictor variable based on whether they scored above or below the median for that characteristic. Subjects were then divided into groups based on the number of predictors for which they scored "high." This approach is analogous to classifying a characteristic as present or not by defining presence as a relatively high score. A person scoring above the median on all the variables would possess all the characteristics. Level of sexual aggression was then compared across each group. This analysis indicated that those individuals scoring high on each of the six predictors had engaged in significantly more self-reported sexual aggression than those scoring high on fewer predictors. In general, the results again suggested an increase in levels of sexual aggression beyond what an additive model would predict.

Overall these data indicated that these six predictors can be used to predict sexual aggression and that these variables, in combination, can have a synergistic effect whereby high levels of most or all of these characteristics yields a higher level of sexual aggression than would be predicted by a simple additive model. The overall findings have been replicated in another cross-sectional study (Malamuth & Check, 1985).

Two Trajectories: Hostile Masculinity and Impersonal Sex/Sexual Promiscuity

In a further development of this work, Malamuth, Sockloskie, Koss and Tanaka (1991) included the motivation and disinhibition factors in a more broadly conceived model. According to this model, the ontogeny of coerciveness can often be traced to early home experiences and parent-child interactions. Family interactions lay the foundation for enduring cognitive (Dodge, Baites & Pettit, 1990), emotional/attachment (Kohut, 1977) and behavioral (Patterson, DeBaryshe & Ramsey, 1989) responses. Home environments that include violence between parents (O'Leary, 1988) and child abuse, especially sexual abuse (Fagan & Wexler, 1988), may lead to developmental processes that later affect aggression against women. In particular, individuals experiencing this type of home environment may develop adversarial or hostile "schema" related to male-female relationships. They may also develop feelings of shame (especially about sex) and inadequacy, which may lead to self-protective aggrandizing, anger and an exaggerated need to control intimates.

A hostile home environment also increases the likelihood that the individual may associate with delinquent peers and participate in antisocial behaviors (Patterson et al., 1989). This may promote the development of some characteristics affecting aggression against women. For example, affiliation with delinquent peers may encourage hostile cognitions, including reinforcing those originating in the home environment. This (as well as some home environments) may also interfere with the mastery of critical developmental skills, such as managing frustration, delaying gratification, negotiating disagreements, and forming a prosocial identity (Newcomb & Bentler, 1988). Thus, being affiliated with a delinquent subculture may lead to the early adoption of some "adult" roles without having gone through the maturational processes to develop skills that contribute to success in these roles, e.g., impulse control. The process may lead to individuals who are more likely to use domineering and coercive tactics when experiencing frustration. These early childhood and adolescent characteristics may lead to men's characteristics that contribute to their engaging in sexual aggression and other behaviors.

Malamuth et al. (1991) suggested that these characteristics may be described in two "paths" or constellations of factors [Note 2].

The Hostile Masculinity Path

Delinquency may affect attitudes, rationalizations, motivations, emotions and personality characteristics that increase the likelihood of coercive behavior (Patterson et al., 1989). A subculture of delinquent peers may aid in the development of such attitudes and personality characteristics, although the general cultural environment may also foster and/or reinforce attitudes and personality characteristics conducive to violence against women (Burt, 1980). Subcultures and societies that regard qualities such as power, risk-taking, toughness, dominance, aggressiveness, "honor defending" and competitiveness as "masculine" may breed individuals hostile to qualities associated with "femininity." For these men "aggressive courtship" and sexual conquest may be a critical component of "being a man" (Gilmore, 1990). Men who have internalized these characteristics are more likely to be controlling and aggressive toward women in sexual and non-sexual situations.

The path encompassing such characteristics was labeled by Malamuth et al. (1991) the "Hostile Masculinity" path. We believe that most of the predictors assessed in the research described above (i.e., Malamuth, 1986) are primarily part of this path. These include sexual arousal in response to aggression, dominance motives, hostility toward women and attitudes facilitating aggression against women. We believe that these are components of a controlling, adversarial male orientation toward females that is likely to be expressed in diverse ways.

The Sexual Promiscuity Path

The second path, hypothesized to be relevant to sexual aggression involves delinquent tendencies expressed as sexual acting out (Elliott & Morse, 1989; Newcomb & Bentler, 1988). The accelerated adoption of adult roles often results in precocious sexual behavior. Boys who develop a high emphasis on sexuality and sexual conquest as a source of peer status and self-esteem may use a variety of means, including coercion, to induce females into sexual acts. Of course, some boys and men may have this orientation to sexuality without necessarily having had a visible delinquent background (Kanin, 1977). Moreover, some males may have a promiscuous sexual orientation without using coercive tactics.

The Interaction of the Two Paths

Malamuth et al. (1991) hypothesized that the degree to which a person possesses characteristics of the "hostile" path will determine whether sexual promiscuity leads to sexual aggression. In other words, the hostility path may "moderate" (Baron & Kenny, 1986) the relationship between sexual promiscuity and sexual aggression. This would be expressed as a statistical interaction. Because testing for interaction effects is problematic when using structural equation modeling with latent variables (see Bollen, 1989; Kenny & Judd, 1984), the investigators first tested a "simplified" model evaluating the sexual promiscuity and hostility paths as "main effects." Supplementary analyses were then conducted to test the hypothesized interaction effect.

As noted in earlier sections, our model contends that factors that contribute to coercive sexual behavior are likely to be expressed in many ways that have a negative impact on men's relationships with women (also see Malamuth & Briere, 1986). In keeping with this expectation, Malamuth et al. (1991) also predicted that higher scores on the hostility factor would result in more social isolation from women (i.e., fewer platonic relationships).

TESTING THE MODEL WITH A NATIONAL SAMPLE

Using latent-variable structural equation modeling, Malamuth et al. (1991) tested a model, shown in Figure 1, based on the theoretical framework described above using data from a large nationally representative sample of male post-secondary students.

This model describes how early home experiences of parental violence and/or child abuse begin a process that, through two different trajectories, may lead to coercive behavior toward women. As discussed above, the first step in this progression is involvement in delinquent activity. This delinquent activity is the hypothesized beginning point for both trajectories. In the first, delinquency leads to the development of attitudes which support violent behavior. These attitudes are associated with the development of hostile masculinity that can be characterized as a style of

- *Figure 1: Model Testing and Replication with National Sample*

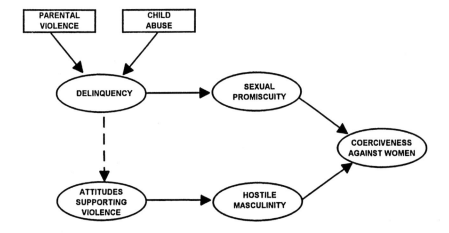

self-functioning involving controlling, self-absorbed, "one upsmanship" personality characteristics. Hostile masculinity is predictive of both the use of sexual and nonsexual coercion against women as well as having difficulty sustaining relationships with women.

The second trajectory described by this model involves the association of delinquency with high levels of sexual promiscuity. Sexual promiscuity, when combined with high levels of hostile masculinity, was expected to be predictive of increased use of sexual coercion against women. Based on our theorizing that sexual aggression in part reflects general coerciveness in relations with women, there was also hypothesized to be a common factor underlying sexual and nonsexual coercion of women. We should note, however, that our theorizing and research has also supported a hierarchical approach (Malamuth, 1988) that incorporates both relatively general mechanisms underlying various antisocial behaviors and more specific mechanisms particularly relevant to sexual aggression (Malamuth, Linz, Heavey, Barnes & Acker, 1995).

Although the development of this model was guided by the theory outlined above, the initial model was refined using half of the available sample and then cross-validated using the second half of the sample. This model fit the data well in both sample halves with one exception: a consistent relationship between delinquency and attitudes supporting violence was not found. This path was significant in only one of the sample halves and is therefore shown as a broken line in Figure 1. This suggests that the hostility and sexual promiscuity paths may be relatively independent trajectories and that attitudes supporting violence and hostile masculinity may stem from experiences other than an abusive home environment and delinquency.

As noted earlier, Malamuth et al. (1991) hypothesized that the presence of hostile masculinity would moderate the extent to which sexual promiscuity leads to sexual aggression. Hierarchical multiple regression using component scores on hostile masculinity and sexual promiscuity was used to explore this hypothesis. This revealed a significant interaction between sexual promiscuity and hostile masculinity when predicting sexual aggression. No interaction was found when predicting nonsexual aggression.

To further explore this interaction, subjects were divided into three groups based on their levels of hostile masculinity and sexual promiscuity. A 3 x 3 analysis of variance was performed with sexual aggression scores as the dependent variable. This analysis yielded significant effects for hostile masculinity, sexual promiscuity and the interaction. Trend analyses within each level of sexual promiscuity revealed no effects within the lowest level, a linear trend of increasing sexual aggression within the middle level of sexual promiscuity, and a quadratic trend of increasing sexual aggression within the highest level of sexual promiscuity. Similar to the synergistic pattern described earlier, the group that was high on both sexual promiscuity and hostile masculinity reported higher levels of sexual aggression than all other groups.

REPLICATING AND EXTENDING THE CONFLUENCE MODEL

Recently we have been involved in research aimed at refining and extending the confluence model (Malamuth, Linz et al., 1995). In this research, we have used the confluence model to predict difficulties in men's relations with women in a 10 year longitudinal study. We also sought to clarify the specific nature of the sexual promiscuity and hostile masculinity paths. We began this research with the hypothesis that the same two path "causal structure" would be useful for the longitudinal prediction of sexual aggression as well as for the prediction of general dysfunction in relations with women. As discussed above, it is our belief that the factors leading to sexually aggressive behavior (e.g., tendencies to dominate, monopolize, control and manipulate women) are indicative of a particular pattern of relating to women in social relationships. We therefore expected that the factors specified in the confluence model of sexual aggression would also be predictive of a fairly wide range of relationship problems with women. In particular, we expected that the central paths comprising the confluence model would predict general distress in romantic relationships as well as heightened levels of physical and verbal aggression.

This study involved following up approximately 150 men who had participated in several of the studies conducted approximately 10 years earlier. Four primary outcome measures were assessed. First, men were asked to report on their level of sexual aggression during the 10 years subsequent to their initial participation using a modified version of the scale developed by Koss and Oros (1982). Nonsexual aggression was assessed with regard to the subject's current or most recent romantic partner using the physical and verbal aggression subscales of the Conflict Tactics Scale (Straus, 1979) and the verbal aggression subscale of the Spouse Specific Assertiveness Inventory (O'Leary & Curley, 1987). Finally, general distress in the subject's current or most recent relationship was assessed using several measures of relationship quality and stability (Booth & Edwards, 1983; Larzelere & Huston, 1980; Spanier, 1976).

We began by attempting to replicate the model developed by Malamuth et al. (1991) using cross-sectional data. This model, shown in Figure 2, follows the two path structure. In the first path, early home experiences, such as family violence and childhood abuse, predict involvement in delinquent activities and promiscuous sexual experience which is predictive of increased levels of sexual aggression. The second path begins with attitudes supportive of violence which are associated with hostile masculinity, which is predictive of increased levels of sexual aggression. Overall, the data showed that all the structural links found in Malamuth et al. (1991) were successfully replicated here. However, one additional path, a direct link between early risk factors and sexual aggression, was present in these data. Additional analyses examining the interaction of sexual promiscuity and hostile masculinity again indicated that sexual aggression is associated with the confluence of high levels on both of them.

Next we tested a model adding the longitudinal data. We hypothesized that the same general causal structure would be useful for longitudinal prediction of conflictual relationships with women. Further, we expected that the two path causal structure would allow prediction above that afforded by Time 1 sexual aggression. The outcome measure of conflict with women used in this model was composed of measures of sexual aggression, non-sexual aggression and relationship distress. With the addition of two incidental paths suggested by the modification indices, this model fit the data well. This again supports the usefulness of the two path causal structure in understanding dysfunctional and aggressive relations with women.

- *Figure 2: Cross-Sectional Prediction of Early Sexual Aggression Using Sexual Promiscutity and Hostile Masculinity Paths*

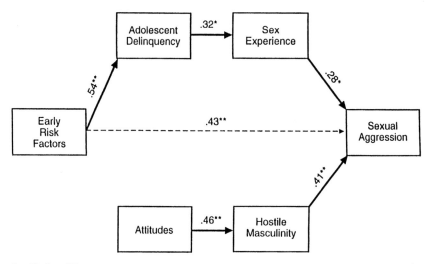

* $p < .01$, ** $p < .001$

NOTE: Standardized Regression Coefficients are shown for revised model. Dashed lines indicate path added based on modification indices.

Having established the usefulness of the model for longitudinal pre-diction of conflict with women, we attempted to refine several aspects of the model using Time 2 measures only. For example, we sought to further explore the role of sex drive in sexual aggression and to examine the role of proneness to general hostility.

As discussed above, various theorists have argued that a sexual motive or "drive" is an important factor in sexual aggression. In refining our model, we speculated that sex drive is not a unitary concept but may include a variety of types of motives. As such, we hypothesized that only certain facets or expressions of this "drive" would serve as motivational factors for sexual aggression. In particular, we believed that the attraction to "impersonal sex" would be associated with increased sexual aggres-sion whereas sex drive more generally conceived would not. Analyses from our longitudinal study generally supported this contention. They showed that sexual aggression earlier in life was predictive of such "impersonal" sexual reactions later in life as more frequent sexual arousal when looking at attractive unknown women and of having more extra-relationship affairs in later life. In contrast, early sexual aggression was not predictive of responses that might reflect a more "personalized" orientation to sexuality, such as degree of pleasure derived from sex, frequency of sex with a woman, or number of orgasms per week.

Finally, we used these data to explore the role of emotional dyscontrol in aggressive behavior. Various researchers have emphasized the impor-tance of assessing negative affect in the study of aggression (e.g., Averill, 1982; Berkowitz, 1990; 1993; Hall & Hirschmann, 1991). We measured individual differences in the extent to which men experience high affective intensity, particularly negative affect, and the extent to which such affect influences motor tendencies as reflected in impulsivity. Such an emotional syndrome in which high levels of negative affect and related motor tendencies are relatively frequently and easily activated would seem highly relevant to conflict and aggression generally. We hypothesized that higher levels of this syndrome would have a direct link with nonsexual conflict with women, which would occur as a function of a general tendency to "strike out" verbally and/or physically at anyone in one's proximity, and an indirect impact on sexual aggression mediated by the specific emotions and cognitions related to women that are represented by the hostile masculinity construct. The data supported these relationships. In our fully elaborated model, using Time 2 data, a construct labelled "proneness to general hostility" showed direct links to men's experiencing relationship distress and aggression towards women and an indirect link to sexual aggression, mediated by the construct we labelled "hostile masculinity." Thus, the tendency for men to experience high levels of negative affect intensity with concomitant impulsivity may play an important role in men's conflict with and aggression towards women.

Risk Analyses

Although the data gathered in our research program strongly suggest that the use of multiple factors enables better statistical prediction of sexual aggression than the use of single factors, they could be due to at least two possibilities. One is that different factors cause different individuals to commit such aggression whereas the other is that the combination of several factors results in such aggression. While some models have suggested the former possibility of "alternative routes" leading to a similar outcome (e.g., Hall & Hirschmann, 1991), ours has stressed the latter possibility.

To test these two possibilities and to examine our model's utility for clinical "prediction," we performed various "risk analyses" in our research program. For example, we conducted such an analysis using the cross-sectional data gathered at Time 2 of the longitudinal study described above (i.e., when the men were, on the average, about thirty years old). For each "predictor," a relatively high score was defined as falling in the upper third of the distribution of the sample. Subjects were then divided according to the number of predictors on which they scored either high or low, using six variables. This approach is analogous to classifying a characteristic as present or not by defining presence as a relatively high score. A person scoring in the top third on all of the variables would possess all the characteristics.

This classification scheme yielded six groups. An analysis of variance comparing the sexual aggression levels of these groups yielded a significant effect. Of the 27 subjects who did not score in the top third of the distribution on any of the six predictors, only 15% showed some level of sexual aggression. In contrast, of the 9 subjects who scored in the top third of the distribution on all six predictors, 89% showed some level of sexual aggression. Those falling between these two extremes showed a general pattern of increased likelihood of sexual aggression with a greater number of "risk" factors. However, in keeping with our model's emphasis on the confluence of several factors, the clearest difference was between the group scoring relatively high on all six "risk" factors and all other subjects. Indeed, statistical comparisons showed that this group (with all of the "risk" characteristics) was significantly higher in sexual aggression than all other groups.

NOTES

1. We are concerned about the suitability of one of the items on Mosher's Calloused Sex subscale. Subjects are required to choose between the alternatives "I only want to have sex with women who are in total agreement" vs. "I never feel bad about my tactics when I have sex." Although such an item may not have direct content overlap with the measure used to assess sexual aggression (which specifically asks about the subject's own actions), it would be surprising if there wasn't a strong association between men's reports of having engaged in sexual aggression and their reports of only wanting to have sex with fully willing partners. Questions may be raised whether such an item reflects an "attitude" or a general statement about the man's willingness to engage in coercive sex.

2. We recognize that there is a value judgment often associated with the term "sexual promiscuity," but we use it here without any pejorative meaning implied. This term and "impersonal sex" are often used interchangeably in this article.

REFERENCES

Abel, G.G., Barlow, D.H., Blanchard, E., & Guild, D. (1977). The components of rapists' sexual arousal. *Archives of General Psychiatry,* 34, 895-903.

Amir, M. (1971). *Patterns in forcible rape.* Chicago Press: University of Chicago Press.

Averill, J. (1982). *Anger and Aggression: An essay on emotion.* New York: Springer-Verlag.

Barbaree, H.E. (1990). Stimulus control of sexual arousal: Its role in sexual assault. In W.L. Marshall, D.R. Laws, & H.E. Barbaree (Eds.), *Handbook of sexual assault: Issues, theories, and treatment of the sex offender* (Pp. 115-142). New York: Plenum.

Barbaree, H.E., & Marshall, W.L. (1991). The role of male sexual arousal in rape: Six models. *Journal of Consulting and Clinical Psychology*, 59, 621-630.

Baron, R.M., & Kenny, D.A. (1986). The moderator-mediator variable distinction in social psychological research: Conceptual, strategic, and statistical considerations. *Journal of Personality and Social Psychology*, 51, 1173-1182.

Bentler, P.M. (1968). Heterosexual behavior assessment I: Males. *Behaviour Research and Therapy*, 6, 21-25.

Berkowitz, L. (1990). On the formation and regulation of anger and aggression: A cognitive neoassociationistic analysis. *American Psychologist*, 45, 494-503.

Berkowitz, L. (1993). Towards a general theory of anger and emotional aggression: Implications of the cognitive-neoassociationistic perspective for the analysis of anger and other emotions. In R. S. Wyer & T. K. Srull (Eds.), *Perspectives on anger and emotion. Advances in Social Cognition*, Volume VI. (Pp. 1-46). Hillsdale, NJ: Earlbaum.

Bollen, K.A. (1989). *Structural equations with latent variables*. New York: Wiley.

Booth, A., & Edwards, J. (1983). Measuring marital instability. *Journal of Marriage and the Family*, May, 387-393.

Brownmiller, S. (1975). *Against our will: Men, women, and rape*. New York: Simon & Schuster.

Burt, M.R. (1980). Cultural myths and supports for rape. *Journal of Personality and Social Psychology*, 38, 217-230.

Burt, M.R. (1978). Attitudes supportive of rape in American culture. House Committee on Science and Technology, Subcommittee on Domestic and International Scientific Planning, Analysis and Cooperation. *Research into violent behavior: Sexual assaults* (Hearing, 95th Congress, 2nd session, January 10-12, 1978). Washington, D.C.: U.S. Government Printing Office.

Check, J.V.P. (1985). The hostility towards women scale. Unpublished doctoral dissertation, University of Manitoba, Winnipeg.

Check, J., Malamuth, N., Elias, B., & Barton, S. (1985). On hostile ground. *Psychology Today*, 12, 56-61.

Clark, L., & Lewis, D. (1977). *Rape: The price of coercive sexuality*. Toronto: Women's Press.

Dodge, K.A., Bates, J.E., & Pettit, G.S. (1990). Mechanisms in the cycle of violence. *Science*, 250, 1678-1683.

Elliott, D.S., & Morse, B.J. (1989). Delinquency and drug use as risk factors in teenage sexual activity. *Youth and Society*, 21, 32-60.

Ellis, L. (1989). *Theories of rape*. New York: Hemisphere.

Ellis, L. (1991). A synthesized (biosocial) theory of rape. *Journal of Consulting and Clinical Psychology*, 59, 631-642.

Eysenck, H.J. (1978). *Sex and personality*. London: Open Books.

Fagan, J., & Wexler, S. (1988). Explanations of sexual assault among violent delinquents. *Journal of Adolescent Research,* 3, 363-385.

Finkelhor, D. (1986). *A sourcebook on sexual abuse.* Newbury Park, CA: Sage.

Gebhard, P., Gagnon, J., Pomeroy, W., & Christensen, C. (1965). *Sex Offenders.* New York: Harper & Row.

Gilmore, D.D. (1990). *Manhood in the making: Cultural concepts of masculinity.* New Haven: Yale.

Groth, N.A. (1979). *Men who rape: The psychology of the offender.* New York: Plenum Press.

Hall, G.C.N., & Hirschmann, R. (1991). Toward a theory of sexual aggression: A quadripartite model. *Journal of Consulting and Clinical Psychology,* 59, 662-669.

Kanin, E.J. (1977). Sexual aggression: A second look at the offended female. *Archives of Sexual Behavior,* 6, 67-76.

Kanin, E.J. (1984). Date rape: Unofficial criminals and victims. *Victimology,* 9, 95-108.

Kenny, D.A., & Judd, C.M. (1984). Estimating the nonlinear and interactive effects of latent variables. *Psychological Bulletin,* 96, 201-210.

Kohut, H. (1977). *The restoration of the self.* New York: International University Press.

Koss, M.P., & Leonard, K.E. (1984). Sexually aggressive men: Empirical findings and theoretical implications. In N. M. Malamuth & E. Donnerstein (Eds.) *Pornography and sexual aggression* (Pp. 213-232). New York: Academic Press.

Koss, M., & Oros, C. (1982). Sexual experiences survey: A research instrument investigating sexual aggression and victimization. *Journal of Consulting and Clinical Psychology,* 50, 455-457.

Larzelere, R., & Huston, T. (1980). The dyadic trust scale: Toward understanding interpersonal trust in close relationships. *Journal of Marriage and the Family,* 43, 595-604.

LeVine, R. (1959). Gusii sex offenses: A study in social control. *American Anthropologist,* 61, 965-990.

Malamuth, N. M. (1986). Predictors of naturalistic sexual aggression. *Journal of Personality and Social Psychology,* 50, 953-962.

Malamuth, N. (1988). Predicting laboratory aggression against female vs. male targets: Implications for research on sexual aggression. *Journal of Research in Personality,* 22, 474-495.

Malamuth, N. M., & Briere, J. (1986). Sexual violence in the media: Indirect effects on aggression against women. *Journal of Social Issues,* 42, 75-92.

Malamuth, N.M., & Check, J.V.P. (1981). The effects of mass media exposure on acceptance of violence against women: A field experiment. *Journal of Research in Personality,* 22, 436-446.

Malamuth, N.M., & Check, J.V.P. (1985). Predicting naturalistic sexual aggression: A replication. Unpublished manuscript, University of California, Los Angeles.

Malamuth, N.M., & Thornhill, N. (1994). Hostile masculinity, sexual aggression and gender-biased domineeringness in conversations. *Aggressive Behavior,* 20, 185-193.

Malamuth, N.M., Heavey, C. L., & Linz, D. (1993). Predicting men's antisocial behavior against women: The interaction model of sexual aggression. In G. C. N. Hall, R. Hirschman, J. Graham & M. Zaragoza (Eds.). *Sexual Aggression: Issues in etiology, assessment, and treatment.* (Pp. 63-97). Washington, D. C.: Taylor & Francis.

Malamuth, N.M., Sockloskie, R., Koss, M.P., & Tanaka, J. (1991). The characteristics of aggressors against women: Testing a model using a national sample of college students. *Journal of Consulting and Clinical Psychology,* 59, 670-681.

Malamuth, N.M., Linz, D, Heavey, C., Barnes, G., & Acker, M. (1995). Using the confluence model of sexual aggression to predict men's conflict with women: A ten year follow-up study. *Journal of Consulting and Clinical Psychology,* 64, 353-369.

Mosher, D. L., & Anderson, R.D. (1986). Macho personality, sexual aggression, and reactions to guided imagery of realistic rape. *Journal of Research in Personality,* 20, 77-94.

Mosher, D.L., & Sirkin, M. (1984). Measuring a macho personality constellation. *Journal of Research in Personality,* 18, 150-163.

Nelson, P.A. (1979). Personality, sexual functions, and sexual behavior: An experiment in methodology. Unpublished doctoral dissertation, University of Florida.

Newcomb, M.D., & Bentler, P.M. (1988). *Consequences of adolescent drug use: Impact on the lives of young adults.* Beverly Hills, CA: Sage.

O'Leary, K.D. (1988). Physical aggression between spouses: A social learning perspective. In V B. Van Hasselt, R. Morrison, A. Bellack & M. Hersen (Eds.), *Handbook of family violence.* New York: Plenum.

O'Leary, K.D., & Curley, A.D. (1987). *Spouse specific assertion and aggression.* Unpublished manuscript. State University of New York, Stony Brook.

Palmer, C. (1988). Twelve reasons why rape is not sexually motivated: A skeptical examination. *Journal of Sex Research,* 25, 512-530.

Patterson, G.R., DeBaryshe, B.D., & Ramsey, E. (1989). A developmental perspective on antisocial behavior. *American Psychologist,* 44, 329-335.

Quinsey, V.L. (1984). Studies of offenders against women. In D. Weisstub (Ed.), *Law and mental health: International perspectives,* Vol. I. (84-121). New York: Pergamon Press.

Rapaport, K., & Burkhart, B.R. (1984). Personality and attitudinal characteristics of sexually coercive college males. *Journal of Abnormal Psychology,* 93, 216-221.

Sanders, W. B. (1980). *Rape and woman's identity.* Newbury Park, CA: Sage.

Sanford, L.T., & Fetter, A. (1979). *In defense of ourselves: A rape prevention handbook.* Garden City, NY: Doubleday.

Scully, D., & Marolla, J. (1985). Riding the bull at Gilley's: Convicted rapists describe the rewards of rape. *Social Problems,* 32, 251-263.

Spanier, G.B. (1976). Measuring dyadic adjustment: New scales for assessing the quality of marriage in similar dyads. *Journal of Marriage and the Family,* 38, 15-28.

Sternberg, R.J., & Lubart, T. I. (1991). An investment theory of creativity and its development. *Human Development,* 34, 1-31.

Straus, M.A. (1979). Measuring intrafamily conflict and violence: The Conflict Tactics (CT) Scales. *Journal of Marriage and the Family,* 41, 75-85.

Thornhill, R., & Thornhill, N. (1992). The evolutionary psychology of men's coercive sexuality. *Behavioral and Brain Sciences,* 15, 363-421.

Yates, E., Barbaree, H.E., & Marshall, W.L. (1984). Anger and deviant sexual arousal. *Behaviour Therapy,* 15, 287-294.

AUTHORS' NOTES

Much of the research described here was supported by an NIMH grant to Neil Malamuth and Dan Linz.

Address correspondence to Neil M. Malamuth, Communication Studies, 334 Kinsey Hall, University of California at Los Angeles, Los Angeles, CA 90024-1538.

SEX OFFENDER TREATMENT
Biological Dysfunction, Intrapsychic Conflict, Interpersonal Violence. Pp. 39-70.

Major Factors in the Assessment of Paraphilics and Sex Offenders

RON LANGEVIN

Juniper Psychological Services, Etobicoke, Ontario

R. J. WATSON

Central Ontario District, Correctional Services Canada

ABSTRACT An assessment is presented that examines a number of prominent factors from the professional literature describing the background and clinical characteristics of paraphilic individuals and sex offenders. The factors include sexual history and preference, substance abuse, mental illness, personality and defensiveness, history of violence, neuropsychological impairment, and biological problems. The reliability and validity of measures in use are reviewed with suggestions for a battery of measures that offer some index of dangerousness and targets for treatment. *[Copies of this paper are available from The Haworth Document Delivery Service: 1-800-342-9678.]*

In this paper, we present an assessment package which can be administered by a clinical psychologist and which results in suggested guidelines for involving neurologists, endocrinologists, or other treatment specialists in the paraphilias and sexual offenders. The assessment attempts to be comprehensive and usually requires two full work days for completion.

DEFINITON OF PARAPHILIA

DSM-III-R indicates that the essential feature of paraphilias is the recurrent intense sexual urges and sexually arousing fantasies involving either (1) nonhuman objects, (2) the suffering or humiliation of oneself or one's partner, or (3) children or other nonconsenting persons. Paraphilics are a diverse group of individuals who have different 'programs' that activate sexual behavior and orgasm. Many of them end up committing sexual offenses because their sexual drive or desires overwhelm them to the extent that they act out in the face of social stigma or criminal laws. Thus, most often the clinician who sees a paraphilic individual is asked to assess the nature of the paraphilia, goals for treatment, and danger to the community. It is rare that paraphilic individuals come to the attention of clinicians without the involvement of the legal system.

IMPORTANT FACTORS TO ASSESS

A number of factors are prominent in the literature describing the background and clinical characteristics of paraphilic individuals. These factirs include such variables as (1) sexual history and preference, including gender identity; (2) substance abuse; (3) mental illness, personality, and defensiveness; (4) history of violence; (5) neuropsychological impairment; and (6) other biological problems, especially disturbances in the endocrine system. Each factor will be reviewed in turn with respect to current information. Reliability and validity of measures used in the evaluation of these factors will also be discussed (i.e., internal consistency, test-retest reliability, discriminant validity).

Sexual History and Preference

Sexual preference is an important concept to be addressed in the assessment. Some men engage in unusual sexual behavior because of circumstances, or for psychological reasons other than sexual preference. However, others have an anomalous erotic preference or sexual orientation that appears to be fixed for their lifetime. Thus, an individual with a paraphilic preference will be at long term risk for offense and must cope with his anomalous sexual desires. This has been recognized in more

- **Table 1: Factors Important in the Assessment of Paraphilic and Sex Offenders**

Sexual History & Preference
- *80% of extra-familial child sex abusers are pedophiles*
- *25% of incest offenders are pedophiles*
- *65% to 80% rapists of adult women are courtship disorders*

Substance Abuse
- *52% are alcoholics overall*
- *57% to 71% abuse street drugs but only 2% to 3% are addicted*

Menal Illness
- *5% to 10% of all groups are psychotic*

Personality and Defensivensess
- *Up to 67% show defensiveness*
- *40% are antisocial personaity disorders*

Violence
- *20% to 50% of child sex abusers are violent*
- *50% to 85% of sexual aggressives are violent*

Neuropsychological
- *50% to 60% of pedophiles show brain damage and/or dysfunction*
- *40% to 50% of sadistic sexual aggressives show brain damage or dysfunction*

Other Biological Factors: Endocrine Disorder
- *Pedophiles show HPA hormonal abnormalities (e.g., GnRH test)*
- *Sexual aggressives may show adrenal axis abnormalities*

Note: Data are from the senior author's database and publications from the professional literature.

recent models, such as relapse prevention therapy (Marlett & Gordon, 1985; Bays & Freeman-Longo, 1989).

As shown in Table 1, sexual preference patterns may differ within a particular offender group, i.e., child sex abusers, and provide clues to understanding the anomalies as well as suggest different directions for treatment (cf. Freund & Watson, 1992; Langevin & Lang, 1990; Bain, Langevin, Hucker, Dickey, Wright & Schomberg, 1988; Langevin, 1985; Webster, Menzes & Jackson, 1982).

Extra-familial child sexual abusers are predominantly (80%) pedophilic in sexual preference whereas 25% or less of intra-familial child sexual abusers are. Similarly, not all rapists (or sexual aggressives) are sexually deviant, although many are. It is generally assumed that sexually deviant individuals will have to cope with their sexual urges all their lives, whereas sexually conventional individuals will not.

In evaluating tests of sexual history, sexual preference, as well as any other instrument used in an assessment, the examiner should always be selecting reliable tests that discriminate groups of interest, (i.e., a test of pedophili a should discriminate pedophiles from non-pedophiles on a better than chance basis). Using these criteria for selection of clinical assessment instruments reduces problems that the examiner may have in court when questioned about the validation of the measures used. It also provides the clinician with an assurance that the tests used do not suffer from fundamental defects that may influence the confidence that one can place in clinical judgements.

Plethysmography

In the area of sexual behavior, penile plethysmography is one of the most reliable and valid physiological measures available. Zuckerman (1971) noted that, of all the methods available for measuring sexual interest, penile plethysmography was in a league of its own.

The earliest device was the penile volumetric measure developed in the 1950's by Kurt Freund and his colleagues in Czechoslovakia (Freund, Diamant& Pinkava, 1958). In the 1960's Bancroft, Jones and Pullan (1966), and later, Barlow, Becker, Leitenberg and Agras (1970) and Laws and Bow (1976) developed reliable penile circumference measures which are currently far more popular because of their ease of use. The volumetric measure requires more training to master than the circumferential measures (cf. Wheeler & Rubin, 1987). Both measures are useful in differentiating sexual preference patterns, although volumetry is far more sensitive and discriminating. Penile volume and circumference measures bear, on average, a 50% relationship (Freund, Langevin & Barlow, 1974) or less (cf. Wheeler & Rubin, 1989), but a number of studies have shown that both devices are highly specific and sensitive in identifying sexual preferences (cf. Frenzel & Lang, 1989; Freund & Watson, 1992) . Penile circumference measures are not as sensitive but, by far, still provide a better index of sexual preference than almost any other measure, penile volume excepted. Penile erection (P.E.) is a function (f) of penis diameter (D) and length (L) or $\rightarrow P.E. = f(D,L)$.

Penile circumference devices only examine D, whereas penile volume devices examine both D and L. Mathematically, circumference devices would be expected to be less sensitive than volumetric devices. Empirically, one finds that both types of apparatus discriminate sexual preferences but longer exposure times to stimuli are often required with circumference measures, and there are more non-responders than one sees with volumetric measures.

There are differences in reporting of penile responses using the two types of devices. Usually penile circumference is reported as 'percent of full erection' whereas volume is reported as raw score or Z score within persons and compared to responses to sexually neutral stimuli. Reporting differences are arbitrary but it is often difficult to have subjects achieve full erections in the laboratory and unsound practices have appeared, e.g., 'ask the subject when he achieves 75% full erection and use that value to compute percent full erection' or 'assume all men have the same penis circumference size at full erection and divide raw circumference change by a constant to compute percent full erection.' These faulty procedures have been introduced because too much data would be lost otherwise. However, use of sexually neutral materials makes this computation unnecessary and also provides an index of baseline reactivity level to compensate for random responding (cf. Freund, McKnight, Langevin & Cibiri, 1972).

Unfortunately, in the area of penile plethysmography, very few studies have reported on the reliability and validity of critical stimuli used in testing, which may include a mixture of department store catalogue pictures and *Playboy* centrefolds that are quite diverse in terms of color and content, the amount of clothing worn by the model, the posture and provocativeness of the stimulus subject, among other factors. It is usually assumed in studies of phallometry that the stimulus materials are measuring a pre-supposed construct (e.g., pedophilia, or an erotic interest in children versus adults) without any external validation if this is indeed the case. Even sexual stimulus materials may differ in unknown ways that can influence erotic arousal or interest.

Controversy exists in the literature about the value of phallometry itself rather than about the stimuli that are used when, in fact, there is little evidence that most available stimuli are internally consistent or are tapping the erotic dimension of interest to a particular subject group. This problem is well illustrated by a study of Sakheim, Barlow, Beck, and Abrahamson (1985). The authors compared eight heterosexual and eight homosexual men on heterosexual, homosexual, and lesbian erotic materials presented in film, audiotape, and slide form. A number of other measures were taken, including subjective ratings of arousal. The results are interesting in that the Lesbian materials were as good, if not better, discriminators of homosexual and heterosexual interests than the heterosexual erotic materials. Logically, this presents a paradox because sexually deviant materials are more arousing to heterosexuals than the erotic interaction of a man and a woman (presumably the prefe rred stimulus). This does not mean that the erotic materials are useless, but rather the materials depicted may be so complex as to preclude clear discrimination of the erotic patterns present in heterosexual versus homosexual men. These limiting assu mptions are also evident in the Rape Index (Abel, Barlow, Blanchard & Guild, 1977), in which the penile arousal to rape versus consenting intercourse is examined. A number of these Rape Index stimuli portray *forced* intercourse versus *consenting* intercourse whereas a number of other dimensions, such as control and humiliation, may be important in the sexual arousal of rapists, particularly of the sadist (cf. Langevin, Bain, Ben-Aron, Coulthard et al., 1985).

A review of the literature on phallometry indicates that there are almost no attempts to determine the internal consistency of stimuli used in the phallometric evaluation. Sound psychometric tests should have repeats of the same stimulus to allow an evaluation of the reliability of that stimulus. Wormith (1985) found a mean $r = 0.67$ comparing 12 rapists, 12 pedophiles, and 12 nonoffenders on 6 categories of erotic materials — male child, female child, adult male, adult female, couples, and sexually neutral materials. Davidson and Malcolm (1985) examined test-retest reliability of the Rape Index in 90 rapists over a 6 day period and found $r = 0.65$, which confounds time and internal consistency. Similarly, Baxter, Barbaree, and Marshall (1986) examined the Rape Index at two sessions in 60 rapists and 41 university student controls and reported test-retest reliability of only $r = 0.26$. Results here, as in other studies using penile circumference, must contend with a significant number of nonresponders, especially among incarcerated offenders. For example, when Baxter et al. excluded 21 of the 60 rapists who showed less than 25% full erection, they found $r = 0.51$. Thus reliability in available studies using penile circumference is moderate at best. This lack of stimulus validation, of course, casts doubt on the interpretation of results when one is comparing two groups, such as sex offenders versus community controls.

There are stimuli used in volumetric testing that have been examined for reliability and discriminant validity. The internal consistency of stimuli used by Freund and his associates has been reported in two publications. Frenzel and Lang (1989) compared 27 erotic and sexually neutral movie clips developed by Freund et al. These stimuli were shown to 191 men consisting of 62 heterosexual intrafamilial child sexual abusers, 57 heterosexual, 25 homosexual extra-familial child sexual abusers, and 47 community controls. Analysis of the tests showed that the phallometric stimuli had high internal consistency (Alpha = 0.93). The age groups of female and male stimulus subjects (age range 5-8, 9-11, 12-14, 18-25) are well correlated with Tanner Scores. These authors also examined group discrimination, a feature that is more common to other studies as well. Typically 10% or fewer of the cases are nonresponders, which also extends the usefulness of the test. Freund and Watson (1992) also examined a large sample of offenders and reported comparable reliabillty and validity indices with over 90% specificity in identifying pedophilia.

It is clear from the studies of Freund, McKnight, Langevin & Cibiri (1972) and McConachy et al. (1967) that the body shape characteristics of men, women, boys, and girls play a significant role in the discrimination of heterosexual versus homosexual orientation and adult versus child orientation.

In Freund's original pictures of men, women, boys and girls, the subjects were sorted according to developmental age and were readily categorized into the Tanner scores of physical sexual development (Freund et al., 1972). The stimuli were all similar in that each subject was fully nude and walked towards the viewer in front of a blue curtain. Each stimulus was presented for 14 seconds. In no case was there sexually provocative behavior. One can say with some confidence that it is the body shape characteristics of the stimulus subjects that are foremost in these pictures. More recently Freund has shortened the test so there are 27 double segments, that is, two people shown in succession from the same stimulus category, in total for 28 seconds. These stimulus materials have alpha reliability of 0.93. No other phallometric stimulus materials have published reliability of this order in the psychological and psychiatric literature. Freund's test materials are highly discriminatory in differentiating heterosexual and homosexual preference as well as preference for children versus adults — that is, age-sex preference. The rate of differentiation for both sex and age preference was approximately 90%.

The picture, however, is somewhat different when it comes to examining *response* or *activity* preferences — that is, sexual anomalies such as exhibitionism, rape, or other paraphilic behavior in which the response of the paraphilic individual seems to be more important than the age or sex of the person with whom he engages in sexual behavior. In many cases, the adult female is the preferred stimulus person and, thus, no new information would be gained from the foregoing age-sex preference visual test.

A number of authors have attempted to generate auditory stimulus materials to evaluate *exhibitionism* (cf. Langevin, 1993; Freund, Scher & Hucker, 1983, 1984; Marshall, Payne, Barbaree & Eccles, 1991), but without great success to date. Part of the difficulty is retaining long sequences of auditory information in memory as opposed to dealing with the immediate visual stimulus. Thus, the listener may have difficulty retaining the information that an 8 year old girl is the subject of sexual arousal. He may focus more on the exposing aspect or the sexual interaction and forget the 8 year old.

There are a number of confounding variables in auditory stimulus presentation that have not been evaluated fully to date. The ability of the listener to form images or fantasies while listening to the tape may be important, i.e., clearer erotic fantasies may be more arousing (cf. Langevin, 1983). The stimuli can also differ in a number of ways, such as duration of stimulus, percent of direct erotic versus non-erotic "setting the scene" material, amount of detail devoted to the age/sex characteristics of the stimulus subject, or the sex of the narrator. Another potentially important factor is the person used in the statement (i.e., use of "I," "you," or "he") which may influence involvement of the listener, although no empirical data exits to settle the matter. Thus, much empirical information is required before the value of phallometric testing for response preference can be dismissed as valueless.

A Rape Index has been popular in recent years (see Abel et al., 1977; Murphy, Haynes, Coleman & Flanagan, 1985) . It is used to distinguish sexually aggressive men from non-aggressive controls. The cumulative work to date suggests that this index is no better than chance. Quinsey (1993) in a meta-analysis has proposed a number of explanations for the disappointing results of phallometric controlled studies of the Rape Index. As Quinsey's study suggests, further work on the Rape Index may prove fruitful.

The validity of phallometric testing itself has been contested because there is not a single pattern of phallometric results for *legal offense categories,* e.g., sexual assault of a minor. For example, only a minority of incest offenders show greater sexual arousal to children than to adults. Extra-familial child sexual abusers may show the largest reactions to a 5-to-8 year old female or may show larger reactions to pubescent females, or to adult females or even to both boys and girls. This has also been considered evidence that the test is not useful. However, results have been consistent over studies showing that child sexual abusers, as a group, react more to children than they do to adults. The finer discrimination of categories may provide clues to further understanding subgroups, but it certainly does not support the conclusion that the test is invalid.

The discriminant validity of the phallometric test has been questioned (e.g., by Murphy, 1992), because the range of discrimination averaged around 67%. In some cases, it appears that the stimuli are at fault, i.e., the Rape Index based on forced intercourse versus conventional intercourse or an aggression index based on physical beating versus consenting intercourse. It seems that the stimuli are not flne-tuned and, therefore, may not tap the actual response preference anomaly exhibited by the offender. However, in other cases, the age-sex discrimination appears to be satisfactory, especially when examined through volumetric phallometry and using stimuli that have been evaluated for internal consistency, i.e., Frenzel & Lang (1989) and Freund & Watson (1991). Thus, two findings emerge from the research on phallometry. First, many stimulus materials used do not have documented internal consistency results and, to a lesser degree, may not have been evaluated for the discrimination of clear criterion groups. Second, response preference anomalies such as sexual sadism or exhibitionism, are more complicated than they were believed to be 20 years ago. We have much to learn about them but phallometric research provides a means to explore in precise terms the nature of the deviant sexual arousal experience (see also Simon & Schouten, 1991; Quinsey & Laws, 1990).

Phallometric measures have also been criticized because they can be faked (cf. Langevin, 1990, for review). Usually faking is achieved by movement, either attempting to inhibit erections to deviant stimuli or increasing erections to adult females ("pumping") which are detectable artifacts. Some individuals try to look away from the stimulus picture but many laboratories monitor the face of the subject to ensure he is watching the stimulus. Card and Farrall (1990) used penile circumference, respiration, and galvanic skin response measures to evaluate faking of 18 volunteers in 108 faking attempts. Penile measures alone detected 45% of the faking but adding GSR and respiration measures increased it to 84%. Thus, faking results is a problem with which phallometry must contend, as must all psychological measures, but is not an insurmountable barrier to diagnosis.

Another issue that has been raised in the literature is the role of habituation and fatigue on sexual arousal during phallometric testing (Simon & Schouten, 1991). Some studies show no decrement in arousal across trials or sessions whereas others do. Of course, results will be influenced by the amount of material presented and the interval between tests. It appears often in the short run that there is a decrement in response within sessions (cf. Freund et al., 1972). Therefore, if one is assessing the relative erotic potency of sexually deviant versus conventional and sexually neutral materials, it is advisable to avoid such a factor by presenting fixed random blocks of the stimulus materials. For example, if three stimuli are presented, they can all be presented in a first block and then randomized for presentation in a second block and so on. If there are any fatigue effects across blocks of trials, it will affect each category of stimuli approximately to the same extent.

Similarly, anxiety or depression may influence the phallometric assessment and some determination of the client's state prior to entering testing should be made. A standardized method to reduce tension and make the client a s comfortable as possible will help, but may not totally eliminate the problem. Not all phallometric assessments should be considered valid. Some individuals will not respond because of mood state, mental illness, or problems of potency, etc. This, however, does not diminish the value of the test. It is noteworthy that in a number of published studies the frequency of non-responders may be considerably higher with the commonly used circumference device, more so than it is with the more sensitive volumetric device.

The phallometric test remains a valuable instrument in clinical assessment. Although it is far from perfect and is subject to faking (this is also true of most psychological tests as well as phallometry), it should not be abandoned for this reason. However, clear standards for administration and standardization of materials are needed.

Other Measures

Phallometric testing is insufficient for examining the total sexual makeup of an individual. An examination of presenting charges alone is also unsatisfactory. One's current sexual behavior, i.e., the offense, may not provide the total map of an individual's sexual preferences, so an analysis of sexual history in one form or another becomes necessary. Frequently, an individual will present with one offense, i.e., indecent exposure, and will be labeled as an exhibitionist or in some other category that relates in an obvious way to his charges. However, there is often an overlap of sexual behaviors that may not be revealed by the charge, but only from the history of the client (cf. Freund, 1988, and Langevin, 1983). Thus, the exhibitionist may also be a pedophile. The male who is involved with a child may also be a sadist. It is therefore necessary to examine a broad range of behaviors and to follow-up the legal information on charges with an examination of sexual history. The tests used should examine for the presence of other sexual anomalies, their relative strength, their duration, their potency for the individual, and if they are orgasmic in nature (cf. Langevin, 1983, 1985).

Standard interview schedules are available (e.g., Kinsey Institute), as well as a number of sexual inventories, including the Multiphasic Sex Inventory (Nichols & Molinder 1984), the Thorne Sex Inventory (Thorne, 1966), the Freund Erotic Preferences Examination Scheme (EPES, unpublished), and the Clarke Sex History Questionnaire, or SHQ (Langevin, 1991). The Kinsey interview requires training and may be too long and unfocussed for examination of sexual deviation diagnosis and preference. The MSI is, in large part, an index of admission to deviant fantasies and thought rather than an examination of the types and frequency of various sexual behaviors that have occurred in the individual's life (cf. Simkins, Ward, Bowman & Rinck, 1989). The Thorne Inventory is psychodynamic in orientation but is not as focused in examining sexual behavior, and it was not designed to derive paraphilic diagnoses. Only Freund's EPES and the Clarke SHQ provide a basis for such diagnoses.

The full EPES is long and validation data on the measure are limited, while the Clarke SHQ has been developed over a 20 year period and examines a wide range of anomalous sexual activity as well as measuring conventional heterosexual activity. The frequency and type of contacts by an individual are combined in 14 different scales to provide a score that is compared both to heterosexual controls and to a deviant sample in each category. Thus, a man who sexually molested a child would be compared on the Adult Female Frequency Scale for the amount of contact that he has had with adult women compared to community sample and, separately, compared to a sample of sexually deviant men. He would also be compared on the Female Child Frequency Scale against a community sample and a sample of heterosexual pedophiles who admitted to their deviant sexual preference. These scales provide some index of the extent of sexually deviant acting out and also of the extent of heterosexual experience and thus, the extent to which the respondent would be adaptable to conventional sexual behavior. The internal consistency of the SHQ Scales ranges from 0.69 for Frottage to 0.98 for Male Adult Frequency. Discrimination of criterion groups ranges from 74% to 98% correct identification.

A number of measures have examined masculinity-femininity, but there is only one *gender identity scale* in the literature that has any validation and reliability data, the Freund GI Scale (Freund, Langevin, Satterberg & Steiner, 1977). The Bem Androgyny Scale (Bem, 1974) and the MMPI Masculinity-Femininity Scale are not as specific and reflect both sex roles and masculinity-femininity and possibly other factors (cf. Sanders, Langevin & Bain, 1985).

Gender identity is important in the assessment of gender dysphoria, i.e., transsexualism, transvestism, and related paraphilias as well as in examining sexual violence (cf. Langevin et al., 1985). There is frequently an overlap of interest in sadomasochism and transvestism or transsexualism. Approximately one-fifth of the rapists seen in our clinic who were convicted of sexual assault also engaged in orgasmic crossdressing. The extent of gender disturbance is important to evaluate since it may be related to the other aggressive activities of the offender (cf. Langevin, et al., 1985).

In examining sexual history and preference, the Freund Phallometric Test of Erotic Preference, the Clarke Sex History Questionnaire, and the Freund GI Scale can be used as the most reliable, valid, and convenient instrument s available and, in the case of the last two, the only two instruments of their kind available. An interview, of course, is essential in conjunction with the self-administered tests.

Substance Abuse

Most men and women in our society have drunk alcohol at some time in their lives. It is not surprising then that 52% of men who committed sexual offenses were drinking just prior to their offense (US Congress Survey, 1987). Some authors (e.g., Groth & Birnbaum, 1979; Howells, 1981) argue that the offender's drinking is coincidental to the sexual offense. However, other authors (including Forester, 1983) consider sexual misbehavior and sexual offenses to be a product of alcohol abuse. This latter position is often viewed with suspicion by clinicians because it provides an excuse for the crime and does not force the offender to acknowledge his guilt which is, in some cases, part of the therapy process. Empirical facts seem to lie somewhere between these extreme points of view.

Reports in the professional literature on alcohol abuse among sex offenders range from 0% to 52%. The quality of the available studies varies greatly and, in many cases, no standards for evaluating substance abuse are reported. Only rarely are standard instruments used in the reports (cf. Langevin & Lang, 1990, for review).

Studies using some standard of measure, such as the Michigan Alcoholism Screening Test (MAST), show alcoholism to be a common problem among sex offenders. The MAST (Selzer, 1971) is a 25-item self-reported questionnaire that examines the main dimensions of alcoholism. Rada (1976) studied 203 pedophiles and found 52% were alcoholics using the MAST. In their examination of 461 male sex offenders, Langevin and Lang (1990) found that between 86% and 94% of the sub-groups had used alcohol at some time in their lives similar to the male Canadian population at large. However, a total of 52% were alcoholics based on the MAST score, compared to 5% of Canadian males in the general population. A total of 57%-to-71% had tried one or more drugs, with marijuana the most common. Although most men had tried some drug, only 2%-to-3% scored on the MAST in the range where drugs represented a current problem. Thus, one can argue that consumption of alcohol at the time of the sexual offense was coincidental, but it is more difficult to understand why sex offenders are 7-to-10 times more likely to be alcoholics than the population at large. It has been argued that they are more likely to be caught than non-alcoholic sex offenders, because of their disorganized and irrational behavior.

It is unknown at present whether more sex offenders are alcoholics or whether alcoholics in general are more likely to engage in deviant behavior, including sexually offensive behavior. In any case, substance abuse is a treatment target that can play a role in the sexual offense relapse cycle and it must be addressed. Rada (1978), for example, noted that more alcoholic than non-alcoholic rapists were drinking at the time they committed their offenses. In their 1976 study, Rada, Laws, and Kellner, found that 85% of alcoholic rapists versus 19% of non-alcoholic rapists were drinking when they committed their offenses. The client who is drinking or who is out of control, may fail to comply with treatment, to benefit from therapy sessions, and may engage in a range of irrational, dangerous, or anti-social acts. Rada et al. found, for example, that the more violent the crime, the more likely alcohol or drugs were involved (Rada, 1978). Alcohol is a much greater problem than drugs because it is more readily available.

Reported drug abuse ranges considerably from 0% to 58% in the sex offender population, with marijuana used most often and narcotics used least often. However, many authors do not report on drug use and it is unclear whether they asked about drug use at all. Moreover, because alcohol use is socially condoned, offenders may be less reluctant to report their use of alcohol than drugs which might complicate their existing court case. Certainly the variation both in the type of offender that one is asked to assess and their history of drinking is complicated by referral source and setting of the assessment, as well as a number of other selection factors. For example, in our own clinic, the proportion of sex offenders who are alcoholics averages 52%. When one selects out the federal parolees who are given longer sentences and commit more serious crimes, the proportion of alcoholics is 72%. Lawyers and crown attorneys will also select cases for evaluation in unknown ways so that sample bias may play a role. The area of the country or the culture in which one has his or her clinical practice may also play a role in the drinking habits of the community at large or in who is referred for an assessment. These factors must be taken into account when evaluating the extent and seriousness of the substance use or abuse being assessed.

Drugs create a different type of problem. Drug use is more difficult to define because quality and purity of drugs are usually unknown to the users, even if they are being candid with the examiner. In fact, they may tell you that they have had marijuana and have had something else, including possibly more dangerous drugs such as PCP or amphetamines.

In the assessment, it is important to know the extent of alcohol and drug use, whether it is out of control, wheth er it is used as a vehicle to commit sexual offenses, or whether it is just part of an overall pattern of disorganization and anti-social behavior for the offender. A number of scales have been developed to examine alcohol use, including the Mac-Andrew (1965) Scale from the MMPI. However, many scales are unsatisfactory because they do not sample reliably and validly the major dimensions of alcoholism, as identified by the World Health Organization, i.e., social, cognitive, and medical problems. The alcoholic frequently experiences cognitive disorganization and confusion, and this is reflected in the global brain pathology that they experience. Social problems they experience that make them socially dysfunctional are family and marital difficulties, failure to maintain employment, arrests, fighting, losing their employment, and so on. Finally, they are exposed to a number of physical diseases, most noteworthy cirrhosis of the liver, as well as other physical complications.

Our own work suggested that the MAST is unaffected by social desirability response set (cf. Langevin, 1985). However, alcoholics are notorious for denying their problems, even though it may be evident to everyone else. It is therefore valuable, if possible, to obtain from the client's physician, the results of liver functioning tests, i.e., GGT, AST (SGOT), ALT (SGPT) and Alkaline Phosphatase. Since these enzyme tests do not overlap completely in their results, it is necessary to examine all three. This provides some objective criterion for the physical status of the drinking client. For example, in a sample of 31 sexual offenders and controls, Bain, Langevin et al. (1985) found that 29% of their sex offender clients had significant liver damage, although the mean age of this sample was in their mid-20's.

It is further necessary to evaluate the history and extent of, and specifics of, alcohol use throughout the individual's life. one should ask about the current use of beer, wine, and hard liquor. The individual is also asked when he started drinking, periods in his life when he was drinking every day, the frequency with which he has been drunk in his life, the presence of any psychotic symptoms, i.e., alcohol hallucinosis, or delirium while using alcohol, about the nature of fights and arrests that may have occurred surrounding alcohol, and about his employment difficulties that may have arisen as a result of his drinking. Although it seems redundant, it is necessary to ask about the quantity of beer, of wine, and of hard liquor because individuals who are heavy drinkers tend to under-report their consumption of alcohol but may respond to direct questioning. It is important not to allow the individual to define himself as a 'light' or 'social drinker' but rather to ask directly for quantities. Statistics Canada provides the guideline that 14 or more drinks per week qualifies an individual as a 'heavy drinker.' Sixteen percent of the

Canadian population consumes this quantity, and only 5% are alcoholics.

The Drug Use Survey (Langevin, 1985) asks about the full family of street drugs that may have been used, and the number of times that they have been used. The survey also asks about the emotional and physical effects experienced during use, i.e., changes in mood, aggressiveness, paranoia, breaks with reality, etc. It is possible, for example, that most individuals who use marijuana will have a relaxing pleasant experience or no affect at all. However, the occasional individual will experience aggressiveness, paranoia, and a loss of touch with reality. The individual who loses touch with reality under the influence of either alcohol or other street drugs may be at greater risk for irrational or violent behavior than one who does not.

Lawyers or crown attorneys may sometimes ask the examining clinician to make a statement about the state of intoxication of the offender at the time of the offense. However, such an evaluation is fraught with uncertainty. It is often difficult to know how much the offender was consuming and what its effect on him was at the time. The effect of alcohol is related to tolerance for alcohol and the metabolic rate of the alcohol (i.e., was he eating, what is his weight, what congeners were used with alcohol, etc.). There is some controversy over the definition of alcohol abuse and alcoholism, but the World Health Organization has developed standards requiring that the drinker has depended on alcohol to the extent there is a noticeable mental disturbance or an interference with body and mental health, interpersonal relations, and smooth social and economic functioning. Many of the clear signs of alcoholism, such as dependence, withdrawal, delirium, and alcohol hallucinosis, are less frequently seen in the sex offender population and usually require years of heavy drinking to be manifested. Sex offenders are usually younger and one must look at the role of alcohol in the *developing* alcoholic and heavy drinker.

Theorists are divided on the extent to which drug abuse is a problem and they have many difficulties with definitions. However, the Drug Abuse Screening Test, or DAST (Skinner,1982) offers an analogous scale to the MAST and examines the disruptive social, personal, and physical effects of street drugs. The 20-item questionnaire provides an index in which drug abuse is no problem at all, is a moderate problem, or a severe problem. The questionnaire asks for drug use in the past 12 months; however, the present examiners ask about lifetime drug use to have an index of drug use and its problems throughout the lifespan.

Some drugs are more often associated with violence (e.g., amphetamines); however, even alcohol may trigger violent behavior, e.g., in pathological intoxication. Thus, the emotive aspects of drug and alcohol use should be ex amined, as they are in the Drug Use Survey (Langevin, 1985).

The examining clinician will want to know if his/her client is an alcoholic or drug addict in addition to being sexually deviant. The client may be a sexually conventional man confused in his behavior and judgement, or the alcohol may be a vehicle to allow him to act out his deviant sexual desires or possibly the alcohol/drug use was coincidental. DSM-III-R suggests that individuals who are mentally handicapped or brain-impaired may be more susceptible to the influence of alcohol, even when they consume smaller quantities. The offender may have increased the dose of his drugs at the time of the offense. Thus, the role of substance abuse in sexual behavior is complex.

Mental Illness, Personality, and Defensiveness

Approximately one in ten of the sex offenders and paraphilics seen in our clinic suffers from a psychotic mental illness. Higher estimates have been offered (e.g., Hoenig & Kenna, 1974), but 5% to 10% appears to be more common (cf. Webster, Menzes & Jackson, 1982). It is common to see depression as a reaction to criminal charges but some men also show this pattern of behavior throughout their lives in response to other stress or as an endogenous mental illness. It is usually important to deal with mental illness as a first priority. The courts also may want the clinician to determine whether the offender is fit to stand trial.

Mental illness is an important factor in only a minority of sexual offenders but its presence is most significant and therapy should be provided as soon as possible. The SADS (Schedule for Affective Disorders and Schizophrenia, developed by Endicott & Spitzer, 1978) provides a standardized interview that offers a DSM-III-R diagnosis of psychotic behavior. In the case of most paraphilic individuals, only a few questions from the SADS need be asked to eliminate them from a psychotic category, i.e., the presence of hallucinations and delusions. Questions on depressive or manic episodes lasting longer than one week also provide a short examination for diagnostic purposes. Many of the offenders will be depressed but fewer will be clinically depressed or suicidal, indicating a need for immediate treatment.

The present authors employ the MMPI (now MMPI-2), which is one of the most widely used instruments in the history of psychology, as a screen for mental illness and for examining a variety of personality traits. The test provides some corroboration of the diagnosis provided by the SADS. It also offers three validity scales (L, F, and K) that provide some check of test taking attitude in the client.

A number of personality measures have been developed from the MMPI and these have been examined by Langevin, Wright, and Handy (1990-a, 1990-b) in a sizable sample of sex offenders. Although a number of traits appear to be reliably measured, it is questionable whether any of these scales are truly useful clinically in evaluating the behavior of sex offenders. The same may be said of the more recently developed Millon Multiaxial Personality Inventory (Millon, 1982; cf. Langevin, Lang, Reynolds, Wright et al., 1989).

The clinician will want to know if a mental illness seen in their client *explains* the aberrant sexual behavior or is coincidental to it. Phallometric testing and knowledge of sexual history are valuable in this respect but sex information may not be available and phallometric testing not possible because of the patient's mental confusion or medication at the time of assessment.

Personality is often evaluated as a factor in sexual anomalies and, at one time, it was believed to be most important (cf. Langevin, 1985-b, for review). Although many of the hypotheses and claims about personality have not withstood empirical test, one particular type of personality disorder is important to evaluate, that is, the anti-social personality disorder. Individuals who have poor socialization, and an extensive history of crime and violation of social norms, may engage in child sexual abuse or other sexual offenses out of curiosity or because of situational circumstances. The presence of an anti-social personality disorder is an important risk factor for acting out. Some individuals prefer to think of the "psychopath" in such terms but the definition of both anti-social personality disorder and psychopath may be illusive (see DSM-III-R). Finally, DSM-III-R criteria for Anti-social Personality Disorder are examined in part through the use of the interview, the SADS, and, in part, from the Cumulative Violence Scale, discussed below.

History of Violence

An important concern is the extent to which violence is an integral part of the paraphilic's behavior pattern, either because he may harm himself or will harm others. Violence is difficult to evaluate because it is not a unitary construct and is an infrequent event. Its prediction therefore is difficult. However, the best prediction of future violence is past violence, so assessment of an individual's potential for aggression is indicated.

Approximately 20% of the sex offenders seen in our clinic have engaged in gratuitous violence against child sexual abuse victims. Christie, Marshall, and Lanthier (1979) reported an even higher incidence at 50%. Their sample, however, is from a federal penitentiary in which the more serious offenders are incarcerated, while the samp les seen in our clinic are broader based and include pre-trial, pre-sentence, post-penitentiary release, and voluntary clients. Earlier reports (see Mohr, Turner & Jerry, for review, 1964) indicated that pedophiles were non-violent, without the benefit of systematic empirical data. More current reports suggest otherwise (see also Lang, Frenzel, Black & Checkley, 1988), so that the potential of the offender to harm children should be dealt with carefully and thoroughly. Of course violent behavior among sexual assaulters of adult women is even more pronounced and is more often recognized in the literature (cf. Langevin, 1985-a).

In the assessment, the circumstances for the arousal of aggressiveness and carrying out a violent behavior should be examined for each person, i.e., whether it occurs in the context of the family, or only under the influence of alcohol, etc. In some individuals one can see a pattern of aggressiveness that runs throughout their whole lives, appearing in childhood and continuing in adulthood. However, for most individuals, this is not the case.

In some clinical circles, the triad of enuresis, firesetting, and cruelty to animals is considered to be predictive of adult criminality and violence. Langevin et al. (1981) found that this triad was not a useful discriminator of murderers versus non-violent control offenders. The presence of the triad may, nonetheless, signal a significant problem of violence.

Pathological family relations appear to be associated with adult violence and criminality. The Gluecks in the 1950s found that disturbed parent-child relations were a frequent factor in the histories of juvenile offenders. Feelings of abandonment, of aggressiveness, and often alcoholism in the parents are the precursors of the criminal paraphilic person as well as of criminals in general. The Parent-Child Relations Questionnaire (PCR; see Paitich & Langevin, 1976) is a 126-item questionnaire that examines the exchange of aggression between parents and respondent as well as other measures, including parent's indulgence, affection, strictness, iden tification, and the rated competence of the parents. This scale does not directly measure the parent-child interactions of the offender and his parents since this occurred long ago. However, it examines attitudes and feelings towards parents and recollection of those experiences which are likely more important reflections of current attitudes and beliefs towards authority figures and the world in general.

The PCR is a reliable instrument that has some validity and has been reworked over a period of 17 years (cf. Paitich & Langevin, 1976). Since parent-child interactions are often the current focus of adjustment in the community for offenders who are released from jail and the focus for many psychotherapeutic models, this inventory serves a number of purposes.

The Cumulative Violence Scale (CVS) is a collection of items examining many aggressive behaviors throughout childhood and adulthood but is not considered predictive of future violence (Langevin, 1985-a). Nor can any other scales be considered reliable predictors of future violence. The CVS does provide a fairly comprehensive collection of items that should be examined in an interview dealing with violence. The scale focuses on *actual behaviors* rather than *perceptions* of violent behaviors since violent offenders so often distort what they label as 'aggressive' or 'violent' (see Lang et al., 1988). Scales frequently ask whether the individual *considers himself* to be a violent person so he rates himself as violent or non-violent. Many violent offenders think they are normal or they lie about themselves. However, when asked for objective behavior, such as, "How often do you hit your wife?", frequently they provide some number, although it is noteworthy that the more aggressive the crimes, the more frequently they lie about their behavior patterns (cf. Lang et al., 1988). Thus, the assessment of violence is complicated but it is a necessity and other sources of information than the offender should be examined.

The clinician will want to know if the client is generally violent or is so only in a sexual context. Is violence often associated with consumption of alcohol or drugs? Is the violence 'driven by' a biological abnormality, such as a tumor or endocrine disorders — e.g., is there possible organic brain syndrome (cf. Langevin & Bain, 1992)?

There are many problems in measuring violent tendencies reliably. To fully evaluate violence potential, all available documentation from sources other than the client should be obtained, if at all possible.

Neuropsychological Impairment

Neuropsychological variables are seldom considered important but research in the past decade suggests that brain damage and dysfunction among the paraphilic population are substantial. The relationship between learning disabilities, brain damage or dysfunction, and the presence of a sexual anomaly is not known as yet, but neuropsychological factors may interact in complex ways with behavior and may influence risk for recidivism and treatment outcome. Pedophiles, particularly, show language-based cognitive impairment that presents problems of comprehension, information retention, retrieval, and application in therapy and in their lives in general. In some cases, there is stimulus confusion as a result of a brain injury sustained in a car accident or other injuries that may lead to acting out, which is out-of-character with the rest of the individual's life.

A number of studies have indicated that pedophiles, among the child sexual abusers, have IQs that skew to the lower end of normal (cf. Langevin et al., 1991). There may be a significant spread between Verbal and Performance IQ on the WAIS-R (cf. Langevin et al., 1991). Pedophilies as a group tend to suffer neurocognitive deficits, as measured by the Halstead-Reitan Battery and Luria Nebraska Neuropsychological Test Batteries (cf. Hucker, Langevin et al., 1988). There are structural anomalies, as seen on CT scans, particularly in the left anterior and temporal horns. The cortex, as well, shows significant asymmetry and less dense tissue, especially in the left frontal-temporal area of the brain (cf. Wright, Nobrega, Langevin & Wortzman, 1990). Other groups, such as exhibitionists, tend to show electrical abnormalities (Flor-Henry et al., 1988) and sexually aggressive men, particularly sadists, show dilitation of the right temporal horn in CT Scans, as well as neuropsychological deficits on the Haltstead-Reitan Battery, but to a lesser degree than the pedophilic offenders (Langevin et al., 1990).

Frequently, sex offenders have learning difficulties that create both negative attitudes surrounding new learning and direction from authority as well as problems with language-based comprehension. Langevin and Pope (1993), for example, found that 50% of pedophilies and 85% of aggressive sex offenders had repeated at least one grade in school. An examination of their expectations in therapy and their interpretation of therapy content was most revealing. They were often confused, misinterpreted content, and were frustrated by their inability to interpret what was said to them.

In a sample of 80 offenders released from federal penitentiaries into a community-based program, 58% showed learning deficits and were significantly impaired on the Halstead-Reitan Battery. Frequently, language-based difficulties were witnessed. Since most therapies are verbal in nature, such clients may not benefit from therapy content in spite of a motivation to change. Many cognitively-impaired individuals are seen as "treatment failures"; in effect, they were unable to learn because of the teaching methods used. Mentally reatrded offenders present special problems for assessment and treatment but they are manageable (Griffiths, Quinsey & Hingsburger, 1989).

It is possible that the neurocognitive deficits in sex offenders are related to some "accident" that has significance in the development of their paraphilia (cf. Freund & Kuban, 1993). However, to date no definitive evidence has been forthcoming to validate this claim, although epilepsy and brain damage, or dysfunction, may be significant in the genesis of unusual sexual behavior (Kolarsky et al., 1967; Langevin et al., 1990). Biological factors should be suspected if there has been a change in behavior after a car accident, or in an elderly offender, or if the offender's sexual drive seems either to reflect sexual dysfunction (e.g., impotence) or excessive libido. One may also see individuals who have been in car accidents or other accidents that have affected the cortex. There may be gross confusion or disorientation, or a change in impulsivity that may lead to out-of-character sexual behavior. The rehabilitation and medical correction of these conditions obviously has a great significance in reducing their risk of recidivism (cf. Langevin & Bain, 1992).

Other Biological Abnormalities: The Endocrine System

Endocrine abnormalities have also been reported in sex offenders, particularly in pedophiles. Gaffney and Berlin (1983) and Bain et al. (1989) found that the GnRH test showed abnormalities in the hypothalamic-pituitary axis in the brain that may influence a number of factors including libido. Disturbances, such as diabetes or thyroid abnormalities, may be associated with behavior that mimics psychosis, with mood fluctuations, poor judgement, and confused sexual behavior (cf. Langevin & Bain, 1992).

Some endocrine factors can play a significant role in the genesis and maintenance of unusual sexual behavior. The presence of diabetes, for example, complicates treatment of sex offenders, unless it is managed properly. Like sex offenders, diabetics in general are resistant to treatment and frequently violate the medical treatment regimen that is proposed for them by their physicians (cf. Langevin et al., 1992). Men with thyroid abnormalities or parathyroid abnormalities may also show bizarre hyperactive patterns of behavior, lack of cooperativeness, or inability to pay attention in therapy. This may quickly change once this disease is treated.

Not everyone can afford a neurologist, or an endocrinologist on staff. However, it is always possible to have a general practitioner who will do sex hormone profiles, hormone challenged test (the GnRH Test), routine liver functioning, and routine blood tests to detect abnormalities in the endocrine and neurological systems. The Halstead-Reitan Battery is frequently used by psychologists to evaluate neuropsychological impairment. The Medical Screening Test (Bain & Sanders, 1985) can also be

- **Table 2: A Sample of Psychological Tests Used to Assess Paraphlics and Sex Offenders**

Sex History and Preference
- Freund Phallometric Test of Erotic Preference
- Clarke Sex History Questionnaire
- Freund Gender Identity Scale

Substance Abuse
- MAST
- DAST
- Drug Use Survey

Mental Illness and Personality
- SADS
- MMPI

Violence
- PCR
- CVS

Neuropsychological and Biological Factors
- WAIS-R
- Reltan Battery
- Medical Screening Test

used to determine whether a physician should be consulted, if one is not already involved. Table 2 provides an overview of the instruments and methods used to assess each dimension.

PROFILING THE OFFENDER AND SETTING TREATMENT GOALS

Once information has been collected on sexual history and preference, substance abuse, violence, mental illness, personality, neuropsychological abnormalities, and endocrine factors, a treatment plan can be developed and risk to the community can be evaluated. The diversity of problems discussed suggests that a flexible treatment plan should be developed. In the case of physical abnormalities such as endocrine disorders or psychotic mental illness, a physician/psychiatrist should be involved to correct the condition before other treatments are started. It is not unusual for an individual to look completely different after medication. In some cases it is not possible for other treatments to be effective until these medical problems are dealt with first.

The individual who appears to have a paraphilic sexual preference can be treated differently from one who does not. In the case of incest offenders, for example, only 25% have an erotic preference for children (cf. Langevin & Watson, 1991), although this is still a significant number and an important predictor of deviant paraphilic preference. In the case of the individual who is attracted to children, Children's Aid Societies or the courts may decide that he should not have future contact with his own children or any children in unsupervised conditions. He will remain a risk for sexual offending against children and his sexually anomalous preference will have to be managed within relapse prevention therapy and/or controlled with sex drive reducing medication. The non-paraphilic individual who may have emotional, marital, and/or alcohol abuse problems may not remain at risk for sexual offenses. This is not to imply that there is a differential success in treatment outcome, rather that the two groups have different treatment needs. It appears unnecessary to reduce sexual arousal to children in an individual who is primarly aroused by adult females.

Substance abuse is also a factor that appears to get in the way of other behavioral changes. The cooperativen ess or ability of the client to focus on therapy issues may be marred by drunkenness or by the irregularity of therapy attendance. A drying out period of three to six months in a treatment setting while incarcerated may be valuable initially, other things being equal, to start on a firmer footing with other therapeutic methods.

Drugs most commonly used by sex offenders (e.g., marijuana) are not especially addictive and are not so readily available as alcohol. Thus, it may be easier to control their use. However, individual attitudes towards treatment, society, and the law, etc., may play a significant role in willingness to give up the drugs. Individuals who use more dangerous drugs, such as cocaine and amphetamines, require abstinence as soon as possible in the treatment process. A number of procedures have been used to deal with sex offenders that can only be mentioned here: behavioral techniques, relapse prevention, anger management, and assertiveness training have all been used effectively. They provide the sex offender with coping skills to effect positive change in his life. A thorough assessment with reliable and valid instruments is a first step to showing that a satisfactory treatment program has been established for the client.

REFERENCES

Abel, G.G., Barlow, D.H., Blanchard, E.B., & Guild, D. (1977). The components of rapists' sexual arousal. *Archives of General Psychiatry, 34*, 895-903.

Avery-Clark, C.A. (1984). Differential erection response patterns of sexual child abusers to stimuli describing activities with children. *Behavior Therapy, 15*, 71-83.

Bain, J., Langevin, R., Dickey, R., Hucker, S., & Wright, P. (1988). Hormones in sexually aggeeslve men. *Annals of Sex Research, 1,* 63-78.

Bain, J., Langevin, R., Hucker, S., Dickey, R., Wright, P., & Schonberg, C. (1988). Sex hormones in pedophiles. *Annals of Sex Research, 1*, 443-454.

Bancroft, J., Jones, H., & Pullan, B. (1966). A simple transducer for measuring penile erection, with comments on its use in the treatment of sexual disorders. *Behaviour Research & Therapy, 17*, 215-222.

Barlow, D.H., Becker, R., Leitenberg, H., & Agras, W.S. (1970). A mechanical strain gauge for recording penile circumference change. *Journal of Applied Behavior Analysis, 3*, 73-76.

Baxter, D.J., Barbaree, H.E., & Marshall, W.L. (1986). Sexual responses to consenting and forced sex in a large sample of rapists and nonrapists. *Behaviour Research & Therapy, 24*, 513-520.

Bays, L., & Freeman-Longo, R. (1989). *Why did I do it again? Understanding my cycle of problem behaviors.* Brandon, VT: Safer Society Press.

Bem, S. (1974). The measurement of psychological androgyny, *Journal of Consulting & Clinical Psychology, 42*, 155-162.

Card, R.D., & Farrall, W. (1990). Detecting faked responses to erotic stimuli: A comparison of stimulus conditions and response measures. *Annals of Sex Research, 3*, 381-396.

Christie, M., Marshall, W.L., & Lanthier, R. (1979). A descriptive study of incarcerated rapists and pedophiles. Report to the Solicitor General of Canada.

Davidson, P.R., & Malcolm, P.B. (1985). The reliability of the Rape Index: A rapist sample. *Behavioral Assessment, 7*, 283-292.

Earls, C.M., (1983). Some issues in the assessment of sexual deviants. *International Journal of Law & Psychiatry, 6*, 431-441.

Earls, C.M., Quinsey, V.L., & Castonguay, L.G. (1987). A comparison of scoring methods in the measurement of penile circumference changes. *Archives of Sexual Behavior, 6*, 493-500,

Endicott, J., & Spitzer, R.L. (1978). A diagnostic interview: The schedule for affective disorders and schizophrenia. *Archives of General Psychiatry, 35*, 837-844.

Flor-Henry, P. (1987). Cerebral aspects of sexual deviation. In G.D. Wilson (Ed.), *Variant sexuality: Research and theory.* Bechenham, Kent, England: Croom Helm Ltd.

Flor-Henry, P., Lang, R., Koles, Z. J., & Frenzel, R. R. (1988). Quantitative EEG investigations of genital exhibitionists. *Annals of Sex Research,* 1, 49-62.

Forrest, G.G. (1983). *Alcoholism and human sexuality.* Springfield IL: Charles C. Thomas.

Frenzel, R.R., & Lang, R.A. (1989). Identifying sexual preferences in intrafamilial and extrafa milial child sexual abusers. *Annals of Sex Research* 2, 255-275.

Freund, K. (1988). Courtship disorder: Is this hypothesis valid? *Annals of the New York Academy of Sciences,* 58, 172-182.

Freund, K., & Blanchard, R. (1986). The concept of courtship disorder. *Journal of Sex & Marital Therapy,* 12, 79-92.

Freund, K., Diamant, J., & Pinkava, V. (1958). On the validity and reliability of the phalloplethysmographic diagnosis of some sexual deviations. *Review of Czechoslouak Medicine,* 4, 145-151.

Freund, K., & Kuban, M. (1993). Toward a testable developmental model of pedophilia: The development of erotic age preference. *Child Abuse & Neglect,* 17, 315-324.

Freund, K., Langevin, R., & Barlow, D. (1974). Comparison of two penile measures of erotic arousal. *Behaviour Research & Therapy,* 12, 355-359.

Freund, K., Langevin, R. Satterberg, J. & Steiner, B. (1977). Extension of the Gender Identity Scale for males. *Archives of Sexual Behavior,* 6, 507-519.

Freund, K., McKnight, C.K., Langevin, R., & Cibiri, S. (1972). The female child as a surrogate object. *Archives of Sexual Behavior,* 2, 119-133.

Freund, K., Scher, H., & Hucker, S. (1983). The courtship disorder. *Archives of Sexual Behavior,* 12, 369-379.

Freund, K., Scher, H., & Hucker, S. (1984). The courtship disorder: A further investigation. *Archives of Sexual Behavior,* 13, 133-139.

Freund, K., Scher, H., Racansky, I.G., Campbell, K., & Heasman, G. (1986). Males disposed to commit rape. *Archives of Sexual Behavior,* 15, 23-35.

Freund, K., & Watson, R. (1990). Mapping the boundaries of courtship disorder. *Journal of Sex Research,* 27, 589-606.

Freund, K., & Watson, R. (1991). Assessment of the sensitivity and specificity of a phallometric test: An update of "Phallometric diagnosis of pedophilia." *Psychological Assessment: Journal of Consulting and Clinical Psychology,* 3, 254-260.

Freund, K., Watson, R., & Rienzo, D. (1988). The value of self report in voyeurism and exhibitionism. *Annals of Sex Research,* 1 (2), 243-262.

Griffiths, D.M., Quinsey, V.L., & Hingsburger, D. (1989). *Changing inappropriate sexual behavior: A community-based approach for persons with developmental disabilities.* Baltimore: Paul H. Brookes.

Groth, A.N., & Birnbaum, H.J. (1979). *Men who rape: The psychology of the offender.* New York: Plenum Press.

Hoenig, J., & Kenna, J.C. (1974). The nosological position of transsexualism. *Archives of Sexual Behavior,* 3, 273-287.

Lang, R.A., Black, E.L., Frenzel, R.R., & Checkley, K.L. (1988). Aggression and erotic attraction toward children in incestuous and pedophilic men. *Annals of Sex Research* 1, 417-441.

Lang, R.A., Holden, R., Langevin, R., Pugh, C., & Wu, R. (1987). Personality and criminality in violent offenders. *Journal of Interpersonal Violence,* 2, 179-195.

Langevin, R. (1989). *Sexual preference testing.* Etobicoke, Ontario, Canada: Juniper Press.

Langevin, R. (1983). *Sexual strands: Understanding and treating sexual anomalies in men.* Hillsdale, NJ: Lawrence Erlbaum Associates.

Langevin, R. (Ed.). (1985-a). *Erotic preference, gender identity, and aggression in men. New research studies* (Pp. 39-76). Hillsdale, NJ: Lawrence Erlbaum Associates.

Langevin, R. (1985-b). An overview of the paraphilias. In M.H. Ben-Aron, S.J. Hucker, & C.D. Webster (Eds.). *Clinical criminology: The assessment and treatment of criminal behavior.* Toronto: M & M Graphics.

Langevin, R. (1991). *Clarke Sex History Questionnaire for males: Manual.* Etobicoke, Canada: Juniper Press.

Langevin, R. (1993). Voyeurism and genital exhibitionism. In Money, J. (Ed.), *Handbook of Sexology.* (in press).

Langevin, R., & Bain, J. (1992). Diabetes in sex offenders. *Annals of Sex Research,* 5, 99-118.

Langevin, R., Bain, J., Ben-Aron, M.H., Coulthard, R., Day, D., Handy, L., Heasman, G., Hucker, J.J., Purins, J.E., Roper, V., Russon, A.E., Webster, C. D., & Wortzman, G. (1985). Sexual aggression: Constructing a predictive equation — A controlled pilot study. In R. Langevin (Ed.), *Erotic preference, gender identity, and aggression in men: New research studies* (Pp. 39-76). Hillsdale, NJ: Lawrence Erlbaum Associates.

Langevin, R., Hucker, S.J., Ben-Aron, M.H., Purins, J.E., & Hook, H.J. (1985). In R. Langevin (Ed.), *Erotic preference, gender identity, and aggression in men: New research studies* (Pp. 181-210). Hillsdale, NJ: Lawrence Erlbaum Associates.

Langevin, R., & Lang, R.A. (1990). Substance abuse among sex offenders. *Annals of Sex Research,* 3, 397-424.

Langevin, R., Lang, R., Reynolds, R., Wright, P., Gaarels, D., Marchese, V., Handy, L., Pugh, G., & Frenzel, R. (1989) Personality and sexual anomalies: An examination of the Millon Clinical Multiaxial Inventory. *Annals of Sex Research,* 1, 13-31.

Langevin, R., Lang, R., Wortzman, G., Frenzel, R., & Wright, P. (1989) An examination of brain damage and dysfunction in genital exhibitionists. *Annals of Sex Research,* 2, 77-88.

Langevin, R., Paitich, D., Hucker, S., Newman, S., Ramsay, G., Pope, S., Geller, G., & Anderson, C. (1979) The effects of assertiveness training, provera, and sex of therapist in the treatment of genital exhibitionism. *Journal of Behavior Therapy and Experimental Psychiatry,* 10, 275-282.

Langevin, R., Paitich, D., Orchard, B., Handy, L., & Russon, A. (1982). Diagnosis of killers seen for psychiatric assessment. *Acta Psychiatrica Scandanavica,* 66, 216-228.

Langevin, R., Paitich, D. Ramsay, G., Anderson, C., Kamrad, J., Pope, S., Geller, G., & Newman, S. (1979) Experimental studies in the etiology of genital exhibitionism. *Archives of Sexual Behavior,* 8, 307-331.

Langevin, R., Paitich, D., & Russon, A.E. (1985) Voyeurism: Does it predict sexual aggression or violence in general? In R. Langevin (Ed.), *Erotic preference, gender identity, and aggression in men: New research studies.* Pp. 77-98. Hillsdale, NJ: Lawrence Erlbaum Associates.

Langevin, R., & Watson, R. (1991) A comparison of incestuous biological and stepfathers. *Annals of Sex Research,* 4, 141-150.

Langevin, R., Wright, P., & Handy, L. (1988) What treatment do sex offenders want? *Annals of Sex Research,* 1, 363-386.

Langevin, R., Wright, P., & Handy, L. (1989) Characteristics of sex offenders who were sexually victimized as children. *Annals of Sex Research,* 2, 227-254.

Langevin, R. Wright, P., & Handy, L. (1990-a) Use of the MMPI and its derived scales with sex offenders, I: Reliability and validity studies. *Annals of Sex Research,* 3, 245-291.

Langevin, R., Wright, P., & Handy, L. (1990-b). Use of the MMPI and its derived scales with sex offenders. II. Reliability and criterion validity. *Annals of Sex Research,* 3, 453-486.

Laws, D.R., & Bow, R.A. (1976). An improved mechanical strain gauge for recording penile circumference. *Psychophysiology,* 13, 596-599.

MacAndrew, C. (1965). The differentiation of male alcoholic outpatients from non-alcoholic psychiatric patients by means of the MMPI. *Quarterly Journal of Studies on Alcohol,* 26, 238-246.

Marlatt, G.A., & Gordon, J.R. (1985). *Relapse Prevention.* New York: Guilford Press.

Marshall, W. L., Payne, K., Barbaree, H. E., & Eccles, A. (1991). Exhibitionists: Sexual preference s for exposing. *Behavior Research and Therapy,* 29, 37-40.

McConaghy, N. (1967). Penile volume changes to moving pictures of male and female nudes in heterosexual and homosexual males. *Behavior Research & Therapy,* 5, 43-48.

Millon, T. (1982). *Millon Clinical Multiaxial Inventory Manual,* 2nd edition.Minneapolis, MN: Interpretive scoring Systems.

Mohr, J., Turner, R. E., & Jerry, M. (1964). *Pedophilia and exhibitionism.* Toronto: University of Toronto Press.

Murphy, W.D. (1992). The utility of phallometric testing. Paper presented at the annual meeting of the Association for the Treatment of Sexual Abusers, Portland, Oregon.

Murphy, W.D., Coleman, E.M., Haynes, M.R. (1986). Factors related to coercive sexual behavior in a nonclinical sample of males. *Violence and Victims,* 1, 255-278.

Murphy, W.D., Haynes, M.R., Coleman, E.M., & Flanagan, B. (1985). Sexual responding of "non rapists" to aggressive sexual themes: Normative data. *Journal of Psychopathy and Behavioral Assessment,* 7, 37-47.

Nichols, A.R., & Molinder, I. (1984). *Multiphasic Sex Inventory.* Tacoma, WA: Authors.

Paitich, D., & Langevin, R. (1976). The Clarke parent child-relations questionnaire: A clinically useful Test for adults. *Journal of Consulting & Clinical Psychology,* 44, 428-436.

Quinsey, V.L. (1993). The rape index. (Unpublished manuscript in preparation).

Quinsey, V.L., & Laws, D.R. (1990). Validity of psychological measures of pedophilic sexual arousal in a sexual offender population: A critique of Hall, Proctor & Nellson, *Journal of Consulting and Clinical Psychology,* 58 (6), 886-888.

Rada, R.T. (1976). Alcoholism and the child molester. *Annals of the New York Academy of Science,* 273, 492-496.

Rada. R.T. (1978). *Clinical aspects of the rapist.* New York: Grune & Stratton.

Rada, R.T., Laws, D.R., & Kellner, R. (1976). Plasma testosterone levels in the rapist. *Psychosomatic Medicine,* 38, 257-268.

Sakheim, D.K., Barlow, D.H., Beck, J.G., & Abrahamson, D.H., (1985). A comparison of male heterosexual and male homosexual patterns of sexual arousal. *Journal of Sex Research,* 21 (2), 183-198.

Sanders, R.M., Bain, J., & Langevin, R. (1985). Feminine gender identity in homosexual men: How common is it? In R. Langevin (Ed.), *Erotic preference, gender identity, and aggression in men: New research studies* (Pp. 249-260). Hillsdale, NJ: Erlbaum.

Selzer, M. (1971). The Michigan Alcoholism Screening Test: The quest for a new diagnostic instrument. *American Journal of Psychiatry*, 127, 1653- 1658.

Simkins, L., Ward, W., Bowman, S., & Rinck, C.M. (1989). The Multiphasic Sex Inventory as a predictor of treatment response in child sexual abusers. *Annals of Sex Research*, 2, 205-226.

Simon, W.T., & Schouten, P.G.W., (1991). Plethysmography and the assessment and treatment of sexual deviants: An overview. *Archives of Sexual Behavior*, 20 (1), 75-90.

Skinner, H.A. (1982). The Drug Abuse Screening Test. *Addictive Behavior*, 7, 363-371.

Thorne, F. (1966). The sex inventory. *Journal of Clinical Psychology*, 22, 367-374.

US Congress (1987). Sixth special report to the US Congress on alcohol and health. US Congress, January 1987.

Webster, C.D., Menzes, R., & Jackson, M.A. (1982). *Clinical assessment before trial: Legal issues and mental disorders.* Toronto: Butterworths.

Wheeler, D., & Rubin, H.B. (1987). A comparison of volumetric and circumferential measures of penile erection. *Archives of Sexual Behavior*, 16, 289-299.

Wormith, J. S. (1985). Some physiological and cognitive aspects of assessing deviant sexual arousal. Report No, 1985-26. Ottawa: Ministry of the Solicitor General of Canada.

Wright, P., Nobrega, J., Langevin, R., & Wortzman, G. (1990). Brain density and symmetry in pedophilies and sexually aggressive men. *Annals of Sex Research*, 3, 319-328.

Zuckerman, M. (1971). Physiological measures of sexual arousal in the human. *Psychological Bulletin*, 75, 297-329.

AUTHORS' NOTES

Ron Langevin, Ph.D., is director of Juniper Psychological Services in Etobicoke, Ontario, and a ssociate professor, Department of Psychiatry, University of Toronto. He has researched sexual offenders for 24 years and has authored *Sexual Strands: Understanding and Treating Sexual Anomalies in Men* and more-recently edited *Sex Offenders and Their Victims*.

Robin J. Watson, M.Ed., Dip. H.S.C., is clinical specialist for the Central Ontario District of Correctional Services Canada in Toronto, Ontario. He has conducted sexological research for 10 years and has authored or co-authored numerous papers in this area.

Address correspondence to Dr. Ron Langevin, Suite 200, Dundas Kipling Center, 5353 Dundas Street W., Etobicoke, Ontario, Canada.

SEX OFFENDER TREATMENT
Biological Dysfunction, Intrapsychic Conflict, Interpersonal Violence. Pp. 71-83.

Comparative Differences in the Psychological Histories of Sex Offenders, Victims, and Their Families

L.C. MICCIO-FONSECA

Clinic for the Sexualities, San Diego

ABSTRACT This is a comprehensive, seven-year research project (1986-1993) on male and female, adolescent and adult sex offenders, victims, and their families. There were 656 subjects, 423 (64%) males and 233 (36%) females, aged 4 to 71. Subjects were either self referred or referred by a law-enforcement official or by Child Protective Services. Subjects were individually interviewed for a minimum of 90 minutes by a clinical psychologist with a specialty in paraphilia. Comparative data are reported in this article on age, marital status, educational level, psychological histories, violence, life stressors, sexual behavior and sexual health. The larger study focused on psychological, medical, urological, gynecological, drug, law enforcement, homicidal and suicidal histories, and sexual difficulties. Offenders (OOs), victims (VOs), people in both categories (OVs), and persons in neither (NCs) made up four groups for analysis. The groups differed significantly on 13 life stressors. The subgroups differed on several factors regarding their sexual histories. *[Copies of this paper are available from The Haworth Document Delivery Service: 1-800-342-9678.]*

The number of adolescent males found to be engaging in sexually offensive behaviors has increased significantly over the last few years. There has also been a corresponding increase among adults in the United

States (UCR, 1990). Males commit the majority of sex crimes, accounting for about 95% of those reported. There is little research on female sex offenders (Davis & Leitenberg, 1987; Dietz, 1983).

The Uniform Crime Reports of the Federal Bureau of Investigation (a compilation of monthly arrest statistics from law enforcement agencies throughout the United States) showed that in 1990 there were 52,108 arrests for sex crimes, excluding forcible rape and prostitution. Of these crimes, 17% were reported as having been committed by persons under the age of 18 and 10% under the age of 15. In addition, in 1990 there were 20,810 forcible rapes reported, of which 15% were allegedly committed by males under 18. Sexual crimes are generally considered to be under-reported, at ratios ranging from 300% upwards. "True" numbers may never be known, but what is clear is that there is a significant problem in the number of sex crimes.

Contemporary research focusing on adolescent and adult sex offenders has been descriptive, and it has indicated that this population is a heterogeneous group. It is composed predominately of males of all ages, cutting across all socioeconomic and racial backgrounds (Becker, Cunningham-Rathner & Kaplan, 1986; Fehrenbach, Smith, Monastersky & Deisher, 1986; Gebhard, Gagnon, Pomeroy & Christenson, 1965; Groth & Birnbaum, 1978; Groth, Hobson & Gary, 1982). Adult sex offenders report their first sexual offense as occurring during adolescence (Abel, Mittelman & Becker, 1985; Groth, Longo & McFadin, 1982; Groth & Burgess, 1979; Gebhard et al., 1965).

Other studies on sex offenders have described types of offenses, ages of victims, gender of victims (Amir, 1971; Deisher, Wenet, Paperny, Clark & Fehrenbach, 1982; Fehrenbach et al., 1986; Groth, 1977, 1979; Longo & Groth, 1983; Van Ness, 1984; Wasserman & Kappel, 1985). Different types of sex offenders have been studied as well as levels of coercion (Amir, 1971; Groth, 1977, 1979; McDermott & Hindelang, 1981; Wasserman & Kappel, 1985). Sexual interest patterns have also been extensively researched (Atwood & Howell, 1971; Freund, 1967a, 1967b; Freund & Langevin, 1976; Freund et al., 1973; Murphy, Haynes & Worley, 1991).

Research has also examined the psychopathology of sex offenders (Gebhard et al., 1965; Hammer & Glueck, 1957; Levin & Stava, 1987;

Lewis, Shanok, Pincus, 1981; Mio, Nanjundappa, Verleur & de Rios, 1986; Ryan, Lane, Davis & Isaac, 1987).

There have also been attempts to formulate typologies for sex offenders (Amir, 1971; Groth, 1979; O'Brien, 1985). Groth and Birnbaum (1978) presented a typology of pedophilia which is widely used. Money's pioneering work in the area of sex errors of the body (the neuro-psycho-endocrine disorders), sexual orientation, and the paraphilic syndromes offers promise as a system of categorization. Money has worked extensively in the area of lovemap disorders, providing extensive research findings and publications with regard to classifications of over 40 paraphilic syndromes (Money, 1980, 1986-a, 1986-b, 1988). Although many models have been advanced, none has assumed a dominant position among mental health professionals; instead, there remains considerable diversity of opinion on how paraphilic sexual disorders come about or how patients with such disorders should be treated.

The present study attempted to fill a gap in the research by analyzing data on both male and female, adolescent and adult sex offenders, victims, and their families. They were studied with regard to an array of variables, including psychological, medical, urological, gynecological, drug, law enforcement, homicidal and suicidal histories. Other variables studied were sexual difficulties, sexual dysfunctions, sexual health and life stressors. This report describes findings from a comprehensive, seven-year research project (1986-1993).

METHOD

Participants

Subjects in this study were interviewed in a clinical setting and completed a comprehensive questionnaire regarding their backgrounds. The clinic provides bilingual (Spanish/English) psychological services, e.g., individual, marital, and family therapy; assessment, consultation, forensic services, and evaluations. The subjects were outpatients and members of their families. They were either self referred or referred by a law-enforcement official (probation officer, attorney, or judge) or by Child Protective Services. They were sent to the clinic for treatment, consultation, or psychological evaluation. The subjects and their family members were individually interviewed for a minimum of 90 minutes by a licensed clinical psychologist with a specialty in the area of paraphilia. The total sample was 656 people, of which 423 (64%) were males and 233 (36%) were females. They ranged in age from 4 to 71.

There are 396 families in the data set, and in 78% of them one or more members had had legal difficulties because of sexual habits. In these families 18 had more than one family member in trouble with the law because of sexual habits, and one family had four.

Subjects were classified into four groups: sex offenders/victims (OV), sex offenders only (OO), victims only (VO), and neither category (NC). "Sex offender" is defined as a person who either has admitted to, or been convicted of, a sex crime or has encountered legal difficulties because of his/her sexual habits. "Victim" in this study is defined as a person who reported experiencing sexual trauma (incest, rape, molestation).

The Questionnaires

The subjects and their family members completed either the male (M1) or female (F1) form of the instrument, an extensive self-report intake questionnaire that covers a variety of areas with regard to the person's psychological, medical, urological, gynecological, drug, law enforcement, homicidal, and suicidal histories. Other items cover sexual difficulties, sexual dysfunctions, and sexual health. In addition, both forms include a number of items that are based on the Holmes-Rahe (1967) Scale, asking the respondent to check the life-stress events experienced during the past year.

Data from persons who could not read or were not able to complete the instruments was obtained through structured clinical interviews. These interviews were, in effect, oral administrations of the instruments. Persons who could complete the instruments on their own, were also interviewed. During these structured clinical interviews each questionnaire item was reviewed and explored further, and additional data were gathered.

Data Analysis

Descriptive statistics for the total group were calculated. Chi-square analyses were carried out with the four groups on categorical data, and

• **Table 1: Comparisons of the Four Groups**

Group	X	N	Males	Females
Offenders/Victims (OVs)	322.72	179	93%	7%
Offenders Only (OOs)		171	97%	3%
Victims Only (VOs)		129	16%	84%
Neither Category (NCs)		177	40%	60%
Total		656	423	233

p < .05. df = 3, constant for every test

• **Table 2: Proportions in Different Types of Treatment**

Type of Treatment	X	% OVs	% OOs	% VOs	% NCs
Number of Subjects		179	171	129	177
Couples Therapy	14.58	8	13	23	18
Family Therapy	18.99	32	18	40	25
Group Therapy	35.24	35	22	19	10

p < .05. df = 3, constant for every test

one-way analyses of variance were computed for continuous variables. Alpha was set at .05 for all tests of significance.

FINDINGS

Demographic Variables

Table 1 summarizes the four groups compared as follows:

❑ There were no significant differences among the groups with regard to ethnic representation. The ethnic composition of the sample was 54% Caucasian, 24% Hispanic, 12% Afro-American, 2% American Indian, 2% Asian, and 6% other.

❑ Educational level, which ranged from elementary to graduate studies, differed significantly among the four groups. OVs and OOs were less well educated than the other groups. OVs and OOs were predominantly junior high and high school students.

❑ There were significant age differences across the four groups. Mean ages were as follows: OVs = 20 years of age, OOs = 23, VOs = 31, and NCs = 37, the eldest.

❑ The groups differed significantly on marital status. In the VO group 50% were married, as were 62% of the NCs. In the OV group, 77% were single, as were 69% of OOs. Among the VOs, 15% reported being separated, higher than the other groups.

Psychological Histories

The four groups differed significantly with regard to having a history of psychiatric problems. The highest percentage was the VOs with 34%, followed by OVs at 30%, OOs at 22%, and NCs at 9%. The OVs and VOs reported a significantly higher incidence of psychiatric problems in the family. Having a history of being in individual psychological treatment was also significantly different across groups, with the following percentages: OVs, 68%; OOs, 59%; VOs, 57%; and NCs, 41%.

The groups differed in the degree to which they had experience with other types of treatment modalities —couple, family, and group therapy; Table 2 gives the percentages.

The four groups differed significantly with regard to why these people had entered some form of psychotherapy. Table 3 lists the percentages in each group.

Efficacy of treatment was not significantly different across groups. There were significant differences with regard to the incident of attempted suicide. In the OV group 26% had attempted suicide, followed by 16% of the VOs, 8% of the OOs, and 4% of the NCs. Victims, whether offenders or not, attempted suicide more often than nonvictims.

• Table 3: Major Reason for Therapy

Major Reason for Therapy	X	% OVs	% OOs	% VOs	% NCs
Number of Subjects		179	171	129	177
Sexual Abuse*	54.50	50	40	47	15
Relationship Difficulties*	11.04	24	18	33	21
Depression*	28.40	26	12	25	8
Anxiety*	19.91	12	6	23	11
Alcohol	6.86	12	6	9	6

$p < .05$. * = Statistically significant. $df = 3$, constant for every test

- *Table 4: Thirteen Stressors on Which the Groups Differ*

	X	% OVs	% OOs	% VOs	% NCs
Number of Subjects		179	171	129	177
Stressor Experience within Last Year					
Divorce/Separation	50.19	78	58	59	40
Trouble with Law	159.53	94	89	48	47
Trouble Law Because of Sex	369.44	89	82	13	8
Financial Difficulties	32.30	23	26	47	44
Hospitalized	9.23	21	13	12	11
Hospitalized Psychiatric	29.62	13	7	2	1
Sex Difficulties	178.63	69	56	19	8
Arguments with Partner	12.24	30	22	39	24
Problem with Child(ren)	151.11	13	20	59	66
Change in Boss	14.84	6	8	17	16
Change in Residence	71.20	75	65	43	36
Relationship Difficulty	65.38	61	50	35	21
Difficulty in School	158.96	63	47	20	5

$p < .05.$ $df = 3$, *constant for every test*

With regard to the method of preferred suicide, the most common, in order of preference, was drug overdose, cutting, and hanging. Jumping off of a building and automobile collision was reported at the same low level of frequency.

With regard to family history of suicide, there were significant differences between the groups. Among the VOs 16% reported having a family member who committed suicide; this was followed by 11% of the OV group and 7% for the OO group; the incidence was 7% in the NC group. Compared to nonvictims, victims tend to come from families where someone has committed suicide. The method of family-member suicide was in the following order of preference: shooting, drug overdose, and hanging.

Significant differences between the groups were found with regard to having a family member who has physically hurt or killed someone (excluding military combat). In the total group 33% came from families in which a member tried to kill someone. In the OVs 51% came from such families; OOs, 27%; VOs, 39%, and NCs, 15%. Across all groups combined, beating someone within the family was by far the most

- *Table 5: Proportions in Each Group Reporting Sexual Dysfunctions*

	X	% OVs	% OOs	% VOs	% NCs
Number of Subjects		179	171	129	177
Lack of Sexual Desire	17.79	13	16	32	19
Lack of Orgasm	30.85	5	2	18	7
Painful Penetration	19.11	1	2	9	2
Performance Anxiety	21.26	5	2	12	2
Painful Intercourse	23.63	2	2	12	4

$p < .05$. $df = 3$, constant for every test

frequently reported. When the OV and VO groups are combined, they appear to be members of families which have experienced someone either physically hurting someone or killing someone. Some of the homicides were, of course, within these families; 4% came from such families, while 6% came from families in which a member killed someone outside the family.

History of law enforcement involvement was high; 91% of the offenders reported trouble with the law. The offenders/victims group reported the highest at 97%; offenders only group reported 95%.

Life Stressors

The four groups differed significantly in their experience of life stressors; Table 4 summarizes the percentages. Interestingly, there was no significant difference on experiencing job stress. The sample as a whole seemed to be highly mobile: 56% of the sample had moved within the last year.

Sexual Behavior and Sexual Health

Sexual difficulties were reported by 38% of the sample. Lack of sexual desire was reported by 19% of the overall sample; lack of orgasm was reported by 7% of the sample. Overall, 3% of the sample reported experiencing painful penetration; performance anxiety was reported by 5% of the overall sample. There were significant differences on the different kinds of sexual dysfunctions among the four groups. Table 5 presents these percentages.

The four groups differed significantly in number of sex partners within the past year. The percentage of people reporting 2-5 partners within last year, the OVs reported 48%; and OOs, 33%, VOs 8%, and NCs 3%. The VOs and the NCs each reported 78% having only one sexual partner within the last year; this was followed by the OOs 45%, and OVs 29%.

Sexually transmitted diseases and illnesses were minimally reported. No one within the sample reported being HIV positive, or having AIDS Related Symptom Complex (ARC), or AIDS. On the other hand only 18% of the male sample and 13% of the female sample reported having taken the HIV test.

The four groups differed significantly with regard to only one sexually transmitted disease, oral herpes. In the OVs, the incidence was 8%; VOs, 3%; OOs, 1%; and NCs, 1%. Overall, 3% reported oral herpes; 2% genital herpes; less than 1% for anal herpes, gonorrhea, and chlamydia; and 0% for syphilis. No one reported herpes zoster (shingles), or candida (thrush).

DISCUSSION

Reported in this study are findings on the differences between the four groups (OVs, OOs, VOs, NCs). The study was done on a diverse sample; gender, age, and ethnicity.

Offenders/victims group had higher percentage of psychological difficulties, having a better chance of being psychiatrically hospitalized and being in treatment. The most common modality was individual therapy, followed by family and group. Members of the OV group, although the least reported as engaging in couples therapy, most frequently reported having relationship difficulty and had a higher percentage of suicidal attempts.

Within the overall sample, 33% came from families in which a member tried to kill someone. Offenders/victims group had the highest percentage of having a family member who physically hurt or killed someone (excluding military combat). The significant finding of lethal violence in all of the groups' backgrounds advises that, during assessment and/or treatment, the level of personal safety of the individual and family members must be considered. Level of lethality should also be part of an ongoing process when assessing and otherwise dealing with offenders, whether they were victims of sexual abuse or not. The findings on the psychological aspect of the individuals, level of violence and the history of law enforcement involvement possibly suggests psychopathology; further study is needed to confirm or disconfirm this.

This research suggests that regardless of the offender group, either the offenders/victims group or offenders only group, one is likely to find that there is trouble with the law. History of law enforcement involvement was significant, indicating that this should be further explored with regard to kind and severity of crime and could assist in assessing the lethality level of the individual should there be a history of violent crime and/or homicidal ideation. It is clear from these findings that these individuals come from problematic families, having involvement with a variety of institutions, such as jails, juvenile halls and psychiatric hospitals.

The sexual behaviors of sex offenders have been described in terms of the sexual offenses within the literature (Amir, 1971; Becker et al., 1986; Fehrenbach et al., 1986; Gebhard et al., 1965; Groth, 1977, 1979; Groth, Hobson & Gary, 1982; Wasserman & Kappel, 1985). However, little is mentioned regarding sexual health — and, more specifically, sexually transmitted diseases, HIV status, sexual dysfunctions, or reported sexual difficulty. The findings indicate that sexual difficulties and dysfunctions occur in a significant number of individuals; 38% of the sample reported such problems.

A high percentage of OVs (48%) and OOs (33%) had more than one sexual partner in one year; yet the percentage of individuals in this study who had taken the HIV test was low, at 13%for females and 18% for males. There were also no significant reports of sexually transmitted diseases, except for oral herpes.

The findings on sexual difficulties indicate the importance of having a comprehensive assessment which includes sexual health status of either offenders or victims of sexual abuse. The finding of OVs and OOs with a high percentage of having more than one sex partner in a year and a low incidence of individuals being tested for HIV virus may imply a lack of sex education regarding preventative measures for sexually transmitted diseases and safer sex practices. The low incidence of reported sexually transmitted diseases may not be a "true" figure in that individuals in this sample may not have been as careful about monitoring their sexual health. The high percentage of sexual partners and low HIV testing are indicators of a lack of positive sexual health. Further research using biomedical as well as self-report data seems indicated.

REFERENCES

Abel, G. G., Mittelman, M. S., & Becker, J. (1985). Sexual offenders: Results of assessment and recommendations for treatment. In H. H. Ben-Aron, S. I. Hucker, & C. D. Webster (Eds.), *Clinical criminology* (Pp. 191-205). Toronto, Ontario, Canada: MM Graphics.

Amir, M. (1971). *Patterns in forcible rape*. Chicago: University of Chicago Press.

Atwood, R., & Howell, R. (1971). Pupillometric and personality test scores of female aggressing pedophiliacs and normals. *Psychonomic Science*, 22, 115-116.

Becker, J.V., Kaplan, M.S., Cunningham-Rathner, J. & Kavoussi, R. (1986). Characteristics of adolescent incest sexual perpetrators: Preliminary findings. *Journal of Family Violence*, 1, 85-97.

Davis, G.L., & Leitenberg, H. (1987). Adolescent sex offenders. *Psychological Bulletin*, 101(3), 417-427.

Deisher, R.W., Wenet, G.A., Paperny, D M., Clark, T.F., & Fehrenbach, P.A. (1982). Adolescent sex offense behavior: The role of the physician. *Journal of Adolescent Health Care,* 2, 279-286.

Fehrenbach, P.A., Smith, W., Monastersky, C., & Deisher, R.W. (1986). Adolescent sexual offenders: offender and offense characteristics. *American Journal of Orthopsychiatry,* 56, 225-233.

Freund, K. (1967a). Diagnosing homo- or heterosexuality and erotic age-preference by means of a psychophysiological test. *Behavioral Research and Therapy,* 5, 209-228.

Freund, K. (1967b). Erotic preference in pedophilia. *Behavioral Research and Therapy,* 5, 339-348.

Freund, K., & Langevin, R. (1976). Bisexuality in homosexual pedophilia. *Archives of Sexual Behavior,* 5, 415-423.

Freund, K., Langevin, R., Cibiri, S., & Zajac, Y. (1973). Heterosexual aversion in homosexual males. *British Journal of Psychiatry,* 122, 163-169.

Gebhard, P.H., Gagnon, J.H., Pomeroy, W.B., & Christenson, C.V. (1965). *Sex Offenders: An analysis of types*. New York: Harper & Row.

Groth, N.A. (1977). The adolescent sexual offender and his prey. *International Journal of Offender Therapy and Comparative Criminology,* 21, 249-254.

Groth, N.A. (1979). *Men who rape: The psychology of the offender*. New York: Plenum.

Groth, N.A., & Birnbaum, H.J. (1978). Adult sexual orientation and attraction to underage persons. *Archives of Sexual Behavior,* 7, 175-181.

Groth, N.A., & Burgess, A. (1979). Motivational intent in the sexual assault of children. *Criminal Justice and Behavior*, 4, 253-264.

Groth, N.A., Hobson, W. & Gary, T. (1982). The child molester: Clinical observations. *Social Work and Human Sexuality*, 1, 129-144.

Groth, N.A., Longo, R.E., & McFadin, J B. (1982). Undetected recidivism among rapists and child molesters. *Crime and Delinquency*, 28, 450-458.

Hammer, E.F., & Glueck, B.C. (1957). Psychodynamic patterns in sex offense: A four factor theory. *Psychiatric Quarterly*, 3, 325-345.

Holmes, P.H., & Rahe, R.H. (1967). The Social Readjustment Rating Scale. *Journal of Psychosomatic Research,* 11, 213-218.

Levin, S.M., & Stava, L. (1987). Personality characteristics of sex offenders: A review. *Archives of Sexual Behavior,* 16, 57-79.

Lewis, D., Shanok, S., & Pincus, J. (1981). Juvenile male sexual assaulters: Psychiatric, neurological, psychoeducational, and abuse factors. In D. Lewis (Ed.), *Vulnerability to delinquency.* Pp. 89-105. Jamaica, NY: SP Medical and Scientific Books.

Longo, R.E., & Groth, N.A. (1983). Juvenile sexual offenses in the histories of adult rapists and child molesters. *International Journal of Offender Therapy and Comparative Criminology*, 27, 150-155.

McDermott, M.J., & Hindelang, M.J. (1981). *Juvenile criminal behavior in the United States: Its trends and patterns* (Analysis of National Crime Victimization Survey Data to Study Serious Delinquent Behavior. Monograph No. 1). Washington, DC: Office of Juvenile Justice and Delinquency Prevention.

Mio, J.S., Nanjundappa, G., Verleur, D.E., & de Rios, M.D. (1986). Drug abuse and the adolescent sex offender: A preliminary analysis. *Journal of Psychoactive Drugs, 18*, 65-72.

Money, J. (1980). *Love and love sickness: The science of sex, gender difference, and pairbonding.* Baltimore: Johns Hopkins University Press.

Money, J. (1986-a). *Lovemaps: Clinical concepts of sexual/erotic health and pathology, paraphilia, and gender transposition in childhood, adolescence, and maturity.* New York: Irvington.

Money, J. (1986-b). *Venuses Penuses Sexology Sexosophy and Exigency Theory.* New York: Prometheus Books.

Money, J. (1988). *Gay, straight, and in between.* New York: Oxford University Press.

Murphy, W.D., Haynes, M.R., & Worley, P.J. (1991). Assessment of adult interest. In C. Hollin & K. Howells (Eds.). *Clinical approaches to sex offenders and their victims* (Pp. 77-92). London: Wiley.

O'Brien, M. (1985). Adolescent sexual offenders: An outpatient programs perspective on research directions. In E. M. Otey & G. D. Ryan (Eds.), *Adolescent sex offenders: Issues in research and treatment.* (DHHS Pub. No. ADM-85-

1396, Pp. 147-163). Rockville, MD: U.S. Department of Health and Human Services.

Ryan, G., Lane, S., Davis, J., & Isaac, C. (1987). Juvenile sexual offenders: Development and correction. *Child Abuse and Neglect,* 11, 3.

Uniform Crime Report (1990). Washington, DC: Federal Bureau of Investigation (FBI).

Van Ness, S.R. (1984). Rape as instrumental violence: A study of youth offenders. *Journal of Offender Counseling, Services, and Rehabilitation,* 9, 161-170.

Wasserman, J., & Kappel, S. (1985). *Adolescent sex offenders in Vermont.* Burlington: Vermont Department of Health.

AUTHOR'S NOTES

L.C. Miccio-Fonseca, PhD, a forensic psychologist and clinical researcher, is clinical director, Clinic for the Sexualities, San Diego. Her interests are in children and adolescents with paraphilic disorders.

Address correspondence to Dr. L.C. Miccio-Fonseca, Clinic for the Sexualitties, 591 Camino de la Reina, Suite 533, San Diego, CA 92108.

SEX OFFENDER TREATMENT
Biological Dysfunction, Intrapsychic Conflict, Interpersonal Violence. Pp. 85-101.

The Genesis of Pedophilia: Testing the "Abuse-to-Abuser" Hypothesis

J. PAUL FEDOROFF, M.D.
University of Toronto

SHARI PINKUS
York University

ABSTRACT Many male sex offenders against children say they themselves were sexually abused in childhood. This observation has supported several variations of what has come to be known as the "abuse-to-abuser hypothesis." This study tested three versions of the abuse-to-abuser hypothesis: (a) the age men are abused determines the age of their sexual victims; (b) sexually abused men are likely to reenact the type of abuse they experienced; (c) men who were sexually abused as children are more likely to sexually abuse same-sexed victims. A consecutive series was retrospectively reviewed consisting of 100 men accused of sexually abusing children. Subjects completed a standardized, semi-structured interview. Men with personal histories of sexual abuse (Assaulted offenders) and men without sexual abuse histories (Non-Assaulted offenders) were compared in terms of victim age, type of offense, and sex of victim using t-tests, correlation coefficients and Chi-square tests. Twenty percent of the sample reported past childhood sexual abuse. There were no significant differences between the personal age of abuse of Assaulted offenders, victim ages of Assaulted offenders, or victim ages of Non-Assaulted offenders (mean age was approximately 8 years in each case). There was a statistically non-significant trend for offenders who were genitally assaulted as children to be more likely as adults to commit genital assaults on children. There was no significant difference between Assaulted offenders and other offenders in terms of frequency of male victims. However, significantly more offenders who denied pedophilic interests also denied childhood histories of sexual assault. This study found no support for an association between age of abuse of the offender and that offenders' victim. The nature of the relationship betweens seriousness of the offenders' own abuse and the seriousness of their offenses needs further study. Sexually assaulted offenders are no more likely to abuse boys than Non-Assaulted offenders. However, sexually assaulted offenders may be more willing to admit to pedophilic fantasies than non-assaulted offenders. Implications for the "abuse-to-abuser" hypothesis are discussed. *[Copies of this paper are available from The Haworth Document Delivery Service: 1-800-342-9678.]*

Many sex offenders say they were sexually assaulted as children (Benoit & Kennedy, 1992; Burgess, Hartman, & McCormack, 1987; Cooper & Cormier, 1982; Freund, Watson, & Dickey, 1990a; Garland & Dougher, 1990; Groth, 1979; Groth & Burgess, 1977; Hanson & Slater, 1988; Seghorn & Boucher, 1980; Swift, 1979; Tingle, Barnard, Robins, Newman, & Hutchinson, 1986). This observation has led to speculation that the experience of being sexually assaulted as a child may result in some individuals becoming sexually assaultive toward others when they become adolescents (Becker, 1988; Becker, Hunter, Stein, & Kaplan, 1989) or adults (Bagley, 1991; Gaffney, Lurie, & Berlin, 1984; Groth, 1979; Seghorn & Boucher, 1987; Stoller, 1975).

Evidence to support this hypothesis includes studies showing a high frequency of self-reported childhood sexual trauma among sex offenders (Anderson & Coleman, 1991; Carnes, 1990; Freund et al., 1990-a; Gebhard, Gagnon, Pomeroy, & Christenson, 1965; Groth, 1979; Kahn & Lafond, 1988); documented histories of childhood sexual trauma in men with paraphilias (Bagley, 1991; Money & Lamacz, 1989); and greater frequencies of reported abuse among offenders with deviant sexual arousal patterns on phallometry (Becker et al., 1989; Freund et al., 1990-a; Freund, Watson, & Dickey, 1990-b).

From these observations have emerged three related but independent versions of the abuse-to-abuser hypothesis: an age hypothesis; a type of act hypothesis; and an orientation hypothesis.

Age Hypothesis

The "age hypothesis" predicts that an offender's age of abuse as a child will correspond to the age of victim he later chooses to sexually assault. An example of the age hypothesis is Money's (1986, p. 21) description of some pedophiles (with italics added) as individuals attempting to

> replicate a juvenile sexual experience but with the ages of the participants reversed. This phenomenon can be traced in the history of some pedophiles who, as boys, were themselves the younger partner in a mutually pedophilic relationship . . . and who are paraphilically attracted *only to juveniles of the same age as their own when they became a pedophile's partner.*

Groth (1979) found a higher frequency of pre-adolescent sexual trauma among 56 child molesters compared to 50 rapists and 62 policemen (40% vs. 25% vs. 3%; respectively). Although there were similar frequencies of sex abuse in the histories of child molesters and rapists if adolescent sex assaults were inluded, a higher percentage of child molesters said they had unwanted sexual activity as children. Noting the higher frequency of pre-adolescent trauma in men who later abused pre-adolescents, Groth suggested (p. 15) that "with reference to the child molester . . . his later offenses often appear to duplicate his own victimization, there are correspondences in such aspects as age of victimization."

Type of Act Hypothesis

In additon to hypothesing a correspondence between ages of offenders and victim abuse, Groth (1979) also suggested that offenders are likely to re-enact the *"type of sexual act performed"* on themselves as children (p. 15, italics added). Specifically, the "type of act hypothesis," using observations analogous to those used to support the age hypothesis, predicts a correspondence between the sexual act experienced by an offender as a child and the type of sexual act the offender subsequently engages in with his victim.

Orientation Hypothesis

The "orientation hypothesis" predicts that children who are sexually abused (and who later become sex offenders) will be more likely to assault children of the same sex as their abuser. A second variation of this hypothesis predicts that only boys who are assaulted by men (as opposed to women) will show a higher frequency of assaulting boys in later life. The orientation hypothesis is based chiefly on two studies showing that offenders who sexually assault boys are more likely than offenders who sexually assault girls to have been sexually assaulted themselves (Steffy, 1976, 39; Frisbie, 1969, 38, as cited in Hanson, 1988, 20). Although these studies provide some evidence of an association between sex of victim and past history of abuse, the assumption is often made that if a man had sex with a boy he is by defenition homosexual or bisexual, and that perhaps this factor makes an individual more vulnerable to re-enacting the sexual assault on another male when he becomes an adult (see Hanson, 1988 for discussion).

The purpose of this study was to test whether information about an offender's childhood history of sexual abuse predicts the type of sexual assaults he will engage in as an adult. Specifically,

☐ Does the age of the offender when he was assaulted predict the age of his victim (age hypothesis)?

☐ Does the type of assault on the offender predict the type of assault the offender commits on his victim (type of act hypothesis)?

☐ Do male offenders who assault boys have a higher incidence of personal childhood sexual assault (orientation hypothesis)?

METHOD AND RESULTS

A chart review was conducted by a psychology student (SP) of 100 consecutive men referred to a Forensic Psychiatrist (JPF) primarily because of concerns about their sexual activities with children. Offenders were classified as "Assaulted offenders" if they could recall at least one specific incident involving unwanted sexual activity before age 16. "Age of abuse" was defined as the earliest recalled or documented age of unwanted sexual activity. Offenders were classified as "Non-Assaulted offenders" if they could not recall a single specific incident of unwanted sexual activity before age 16 or if they said they "didn't know" or "couldn't remember" being sexually abused. "Offender abuse age" was defined as the earliest age the offender recalled being sexually abused himself (all offenders in this sample who reported being sexually assaulted said it happened before they were 16). "Victim abuse age" was

• *Table 1: Characteristics of Subjects*

	Assaulted Offenders	Non-Assaulted Offenders
Number of Subjects	20	80
Marital Status		
Single	30%	40%
Married/Common-law	45%	40%
Divorced/Separated	25%	20%
Race		
White	93%	89%
Other	7%	11%
Employment Status		
Employed	80%	74%
Unemployed	20%	26%
Socioeconomic Status[1]		
Levels I-II	5%	7%
Levels III-V	95%	93%
Gender of Victim		
Male	25%	34%
Female	65%	63%
Both	10%	4%
Relationship to Victim		
Family member	67%	59%
Acquaintance	22%	29%
Stranger	11%	12%

[1]*According to Hollingshead's criteria (1958).*

There were no significant differences on Chi^2 between the groups on any of the variables listed.

defined as the age of the offender's first vicitm at the time of the victim's first sexual assault by the offender. Of the 100 subjects, 4 claimed they had only pedophilic fantasies (that is, they said they had never actually acted on any of their sexual urges for children). In these cases, the victim's abuse age was taken as the age of the victim in the subject's preferred pedophilic sexual fantasy.

Data were reported in terms of means and standard deviations (positive and negative), along with frequency counts. Unless otherwise stated,

FIGURE 1

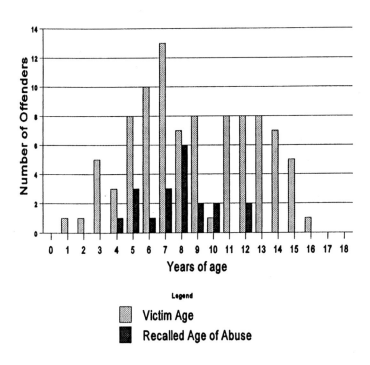

Histogram frequency count of the ages of offenders victims and ages of offenders recalled abuse.

parametric data were compared using un-paired 2-tailed t-tests and Pearson product-moment correlations. Non-parametric data were compared using Chi-square tests.

Demographic Variables

There were 20 Assaulted offenders and 80 Non-Assaulted offenders in the study sample. There were no significant differences between Assaulted and Non-Assaulted offenders in terms of age (36 +/- 10 years vs. 40 +/- 14 years, respectively); education (11 +/- 4 years vs. 11 +/- 3 years, respectively), number of children (1.5 +/- 1 children vs. 1.5 +/- 2 children, respectively); or number of victims (2.8 +/- 4 victims vs. 1.9 +/- 3 victims, respectively).

There was no significant difference between the mean victim abuse ages of the Assaulted offenders and Non-Assaulted offenders (8.6 +/- 4.6 years vs. 8.6 +/- 3.7 years respectively; unpaired $t = 0$, $df = 98$, $p = NS$). There were no significant differences between the two groups on any of the categorical demographic variables shown in Table 1. The only categorical variable that differed between the two groups was whether or not the offenders admitted having pedophilic fantasies.

At the time of assessment, only one of 20 Assaulted offenders (5%) attempted to deny having any pedophilic sexual arousal compared to 29 out of 80 (38%) of Non-Assaulted offenders ($Chi^2 = 7.9$, $df = 1$, $p = 0.005$).

Age of Abuse

The age of abuse hypothesis hypothesis predicts that the offender abuse age will be similar to the victim age. In the group of Assaulted offenders ($N = 20$), abuse age was similar to victim age (8.5 +/- 4.6 years vs. 7.8 +/- 2.2 years, respectively). A histogram indicating the number of offenders who had vicitms at each year of age ($N = 100$) together with the number of offenders abused at each year of age ($N = 20$) is shown in Figure 1.

However, when abuse age and victim age were compared using the appropriate *paired* t-test, the mean difference in offender abuse ages and victim abuse ages was 6.7 years (paired $t = -11.8$, $df = 39$, $p = 0.0001$) and the Product-moment correllation for these 2 variables was not significant ($r^2 = 0.018$, $p = NS$). The relationship between the offenders' abuse ages and their first victims' abuse ages is shown in Figure 2. In fact, only one of 20 Assaulted offenders (5%) had abuse ages equal to within one year of their victim's abuse ages.

FIGURE 2

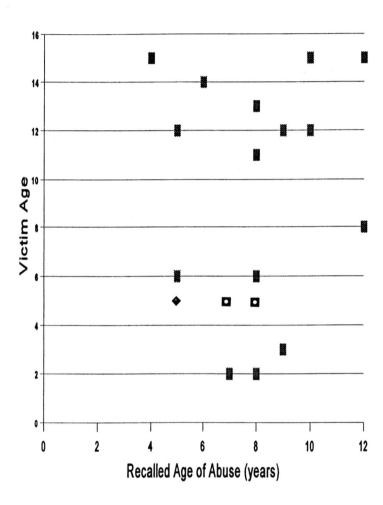

Scattergram of offenders recalled age of abuse vs. known age of victims ($r^2 = 0.018$, p = NS). ◆ indicates the single offender whose age of abuse was the same as his victim's age. ◻ indicates two offenders.

Given the large mean difference in offender abuse age and victim abuse age in the Assaulted offender group, the analysis was repeated using the wider age categories employed by Groth (1979). However, when this was done, offenders assaulted during preschool (1 through 6 years; N = 5), preadolescence (7 through 12 years; N = 15), or adolescence (13 through 15 years; N = 0), did not have significantly more victims in the corresponding age category than offenders assaulted in the other two categories ($Chi^2 = 0.8$, df = 2, p = NS).

Finally, the age hypothesis predicts that offenders with younger than average victims should have younger than average offender abuse ages.

Conversely, offenders with older than average vicitms should have older than average offender abuse ages. To test this prediction, the sub-group of offenders with victim abuse ages that were more than one standard deviation from the mean victim abuse age were selected. There were eight Assaulted offenders who met this criteria but the correlation between their victim's age and the age the offenders were assaulted was also non-significant ($r^2 = 0.073$, p = NS).

Type of Offense

Due to the small sample size, sexual acts were divided into only 2 categories for analysis: "Manual assault" and "Genital assault." Manual assault was defined as assaults that included any sexually inappropriate activity that did not proceed beyond touching of the genitals or anal region with a hand. Genital assault was defined as any sexual activity that involved genital or anal touching with the adult's penis or mouth. Within the Assaulted offender group, 8 of 10 men (80%) who had been manually assaulted committed manual assaults on their victims. Similarly, 7 of 10 men (70%) who had been genitally assaulted in turn genitally assaulted their victims ($Chi^2 = 5.1$, df = 1, p = 0.02). However, this result was non-significant when statistically corrected to account for the small expected frequencies using Fisher's Exact test (Pearson & Hartley, 1966).

Orientation of Offenders

The orientation hypothesis predicts that men who assault boys are more likely, when they were young, to have been assualted by men themselves. However, in this sample there was no significant difference between Assaulted and Non-Assaulted offenders in terms of the percent who assaulted males only (25% vs. 34%, respectively); females only (65% vs. 63%, respectively); or both sexes (10% vs. 4%, respectively; $Chi^2 = 1.6$, df = 2, p = NS).

Next, the relationship between sex of the individual who sexually assaulted the offender and the offender's victim was compared. Among Assaulted offenders in this sample, 6 of 15 men who had been assaulted by men (40%) had male victims compared to three of four men who had been assaulted by women (75%) and who in turn assaulted female victims ($Chi^2 = 0.65$, df = 1, p = NS; one offender was excluded from this analysis because he recalled being assaulted by both a male and female assailant). A correlation between the age of abuse and age of victim for offenders who themselves had been assaulted as children by men was non-significant ($r^2 = 0.002$, p = NS).

Finally, the relationship between sex of victim and the offender's self-identified sexual orientation was examined. In this sample of 100 men, 83% identified themselves as heterosexual, 5% identified themselves as homosexual, and 12% identified themselves as bisexual or "unable to decide." Men who considered themselves heterosexual assaulted male victims in 28% of the cases. Men who considered themselves homosexual assaulted female victims in 20% of the cases. Men who considered themselves bisexual had male victims in 84% of the cases and female victims in 16% of the cases. Of the Assaulted offender sub-sample, 17 (85%) identified themselves as heterosexual, 3 (15%) identified themselves as bisexual and there were no offenders in this group who considered themselves homosexual.

DISCUSSION

Limitations

This study shares many of the limitations of previous studies on this topic, the most important of which is the fact that it is retrospective and examined males only. To the authors' knowledge there have been only 2 prospective studies specifically addressing the issue of paraphilic behavior resulting from early sexual assaults. Burgess et al. (1987) reported on the results of a 6-8 year follow-up of 34 "young people" from two "sex rings" involved in the production of child pornography by adults. No significant differences in sexual interests and behavior were found between sexually abused youngsters and their controls from the first sex ring and the abused young people in the second sex ring differed from controls only in terms of "compulsive masturbation" and prostitution. Although one of the subjects had been convicted of sex with a juvenile, the authors primarily discussed the relationship between sexual abuse and later drug abuse, juvenile delinquency, and (non-sexual) criminal behavior.

Money and Lamacz (1989) reported on their longitudinal study of seven patients with ambiguous genitalia or endocrine abnormalities diagnosed at birth who developed paraphilias. Unfortunately, in addition to sexual trauma, the patients in this study all suffered physical and emotional abuse making it impossible to attribute their paraphilic interests solely to sexual abuse.

While the design of the present study is not sufficient to prove the abuse-to-abuser hypothesis, it is sufficient to test the specific predictions of the hypothesis regarding age, type of act and orientation. However, the sample size of this study limits the power of the conclusions as well as the generalizability of the conclusions.

Additional short-comings of this study include the fact that the major source of information about the childhood sexual abuse histories of offenders is the offender himself. Convicted offenders may exaggerate their sexual abuse histories in the hopes of mitigating or justifying their crimes (Freund et al., 1990-a; Hindeman, 1988). They may also be more likely to remember unusual sexual experiences, particularly if they have been through therapy designed to encourage recollection and reporting of past sexual activities (Fedoroff, 1992; Loftus, 1993). However, the methods of determining sexual abuse histories in this study are comparable to methods used in studies which have been interpreted as supporting the abuse-to-abuser hypothesis.

Finally, experiences of sexual assault may be more likely to co-occur with other variables such as familial mental illness (Bagley, 1991), alcoholism (Peters, 1976; Rada, 1976), adoption (Russell, 1986), and physical or emotional abuse (Burgess et al., 1987). This makes any final conclusion about a direct relationship between sexual abuse and sexual assault very difficult since childhood experiences of sexual assault and adult sex offenses may simply be epi-phenomena (independent occurrences that are frequent enough so as to appear to be causally related in certain populations). This is particularly true since sexual assault often occurs together with physical and emotional abuse which themselves may have inter-generational patterns (Oliver, 1993). Given these cautions, several findings were nonetheless of interest, as explicated below.

Age Hypothesis

The major finding of this study was the absence of a correlation between the offender abuse age and the age of abuse for their victims. There were no significant differences between the group mean age of offender abuse, the group mean age of Assaulted offenders' victims, or the group mean age of Non-Assaulted offenders' victims. All three mean ages of abuse were at approximately age 8 years of age.

However, on paired t-tests, offenders' age of abuse was significantly different from their victims' age of abuse. In addition, among Assaulted offenders, those with younger or older victims than average failed to have victims who were younger or older than average as would be predicted by the abuse-to-abuser age hypothesis.

Together these findings indicate no direct relationship between the age an offender is assaulted and the age of his victim. In addition, these findings suggest that one of the reasons the age hypothesis has been accepted in the past is because the mean age of offender abuse happens to be the same as the mean age of victim abuse by virtue of the fact that the median age of being a child is age 8 (half-way between 0 and 16). This would make the correspondence between age of abuse and age of victim likely even though there may be no direct relationship.

Type of Offense Hypothesis

This study found weak support for the type of offense hypothesis by showing that genital assaults were committed more frequently by men who had been genitally assaulted themselves compared to men who had suffered only manual assault. However, this finding was not statistically significant when corrected for sample size. In addition, this finding is dependent on the accuracy of the recollection of offenders who may be more likely to exaggerate the extent of their own assaults if they are accused of more serious genital offenses. This possibility is supported by the present study's finding that significantly more offenders who admitted having pedophilic interests also reported a significantly higher frequency of sex abuse during childhood. A similar finding has been reported by Freund et al. (1990-a).

There are two explanations for this finding. Men abused in childhood may indeed be more pedophilic than Non-Abused offenders. Alternatively, men accused of pedophilia may believe the abuse-to-abuser hypothesis and think that admitting to having been abused as a child will incriminate them. If this is so, it could be predicted that men attempting to deny pedophilic interests will also conceal information about past sex assault. Unfortunately, the design of this study does not allow a determination of which interpretation is correct. Therefore, these findings need further research with a larger sample in which objective measures of pedophilia are available, preferably one in which type of abuse can be more finely categorized and externally validated.

Orientation Hypothesis

Previous studies have reported a higher frequency of personal childhood abuse among sex offenders who assault boys (Hanson & Slater, 1988). Some clinicians have interpreted this finding to mean that homosexual men who were themselves assaulted by men are more likely to assault boys than other offenders.

However, this study found that sex of victim does not correspond to the offender's self-reported sexual orientation in 37% of cases (homosexuals assaulting females or heterosexuals assaulting males). Studies that make presumptions about the sexual orientation of offenders based solely on the sex of the victim may therefore be mis-assigning a third of the cases.

In this sample, there was no significant difference between Assaulted offenders and Non-Assaulted offenders in either sexual orientation or frequency of male victims. These findings together with the finding that the majority of sexual assaults in this sample were committed by men who considered themselves heterosexual and who were not assaulted, suggests there is no evidence from this study to support a relationship between history of sexual assault as a child, homosexuality, or sex of victim in male sex offenders against children.

CONCLUSIONS

Since the abuse-to-abuser hypothesis for pedophilia is based upon retrospective studies of men, there is no evidence to prove a causal relationship. This study found no evidence to support even a weak correlation between age of offender abuse and age of victim abuse. Future studies should control for spuriously significant results due to the fact that group means and medians for offender abuse age and victim abuse age are likely to cluster around age 8 for statistical reasons.

This study found weak support for the hypothesis that offenders may be more likely to re-enact the same type of sexual abuse they received. However, this finding may be due to the small sample size and selective reporting. Prospective or follow-up studies of children with documented sexual abuse are needed to verify this hypothesis.

There was no evidence in this study that men who were sexually assaulted would be more likely to identify themselves as homosexual or to choose male victims. Retrospective studies of the association between sexual abuse, sexual orientation, and sex of victim that are based on self-reported histories of sexual abuse and sex of victim are not sufficient to prove a causal relationship between these variables.

Finally, although there was little support for the abuse-to-abuser hypothesis in this sample, this study does not rule out the possibility that there is a specific sub-group of sex offenders who do show a relationship between the age of their own sexual abuse and that of their victims. In this study, only one of 100 male sex offenders (1%) was found to have been sexually abused at the same age as their victims. This study suggests that such people are rare but they would certainly be of interest for further studies aimed at demonstrating what factors (if any) cause such a relationship to develop.

SUMMARY

We conclude that the only portion of the abuse-to-abuser hypothesis that was weakly supported by this study is the Type of act hypothesis. The finding that men who continued to deny pedophilic activities had a significantly lower frequency of reported personal childhood sexual abuse raises the possibility that sex offenders themselves believe in the abuse-to-abuser hypothesis and think that disclosing past sexual assaults on them may incriminate them. Further studies of convicted men who deny sex offenses should be conducted to replicate this finding. Until further evidence is available the abuse-to-abuser hypothesis for pedophilia should be considered unverified.

REFERENCES

Anderson, N. B., & Coleman, E. (1991). Childhood abuse and family sexual attitudes in sexually compulsive males: A comparison of three clinical groups..*American Journal of Preventive Psychiatry and Neurology*, 3 (1), 8-15.

Bagley, C. (1991). The long-term psychological effects of child sexual abuse: A review of some British and Canadian studies of victims and their families..*Annals of Sex Research,* 4, 23-48.

Becker, J.V. (1988). The effects of child sexual abuse on adolescent sexual offenders. In G.Wyatt & G.Powell (Eds.), *Lasting effects of child sexual abuse* (pp.193-208). Newbury Park, CA: Sage.

Becker, J.V., Hunter, J.A., Stein, R.N., & Kaplan, N.S. (1989). Factors associated with erection in adolescent sex offenders. *Psychopathology and Behavioral Assessment,* 11, 353-362.

Benoit, J.L., & Kennedy, W. (1992). The abuse history of male adolescent sex offenders..*Journal of Interpersonal Violence,* 7 (4), 543-548.

Burgess, A.W., Hartman, C.R., & McCormack, A. (1987). Abused to abuser: Antecedents of socially deviant behaviors. *American Journal of Psychiatry,* 144 (11), 1431-1436.

Carnes, P. (1990). Sexual addiction: progress, criticism, challenges. *American Journal of Preventive Psychiatry and Neurology,* 2, 1-8.

Cooper, I., & Cormier, B. (1982). Inter-generational transmission of incest. *Canadian Journal of Psychiatry*, 27, 231-235.

Fedoroff, J.P., Hanson, A., McGuire, M., Malin, H.M., and Berlin, F.S. 1992. Simulated paraphilias: A preliminary study of patients who imitate or exaggerate paraphilic symptoms and behaviors..*Journal of Forensic Sciences,* 37 (3), 19-32.

Freund, K.,Watson, R., & Dickey, R. (1990-a). Does sexual abuse in childhood cause pedophilia: An exploratory study. *Archives of Sexual Behavior*, 19 (6), 557-568.

Freund, K.,Watson, R., & Dickey, R. (1990-b). Sex offenses against female children perpetrated by men who are not pedophiles. *Journal of Sex Research,* 28 (3), 402-423.

Gaffney, G.R., Lurie, S.F., & Berlin, F.S. (1984). Is there familial transmission of pedophilia? *Journal of Nervous and Mental Disease,* 172 (9), 546-548.

Garland, R., & Dougher, M. (1990). The abused/abuser hypothesis of child abuse: A critical review of theory and research. In J.R.Feierman (Ed.), *Pedophilia: Biosocial Dimensions* (Pp. 488-509). New York: Springer-Verlag.

Gebhard, P.H., Gagnon, J.H., Pomeroy, W.B., & Christenson, C.V. (1965). *Sex offenders.An analysis of types.* London: William Heinemann.

Groth, A.N. (1979). Sexual trauma in the life histories of rapists and child molesters.*Victimology,* 4 (1), 10-16.

Groth, A.N., & Burgess, A.W. (1977). Motivational intent in the sexual assault on children. *Criminal Justice and Behavior,* 4, 253-264.

Hanson, R.K., & Slater, S. (1988). Sexual victimization in the history of child sexual abusers: a review. *Annals of Sex Research*, 1, 485-499.

Hindeman, J. (1988). Research disputes assumptions about child molesters. *NDAA Bulletin,* 7, 1-3.

Kahn, T.J., & Lafond, M.A. (1988). Treatment of the adolescent sexual offender. *Child and Adolescent Social Work,* 5, 135-148.

Loftus, E.F. (1993). The reality of repressed memories. *American Psychologist,* 48 (5), 518-537.

Money, J., & Lamacz, M. (1989). *Vandalized Lovemaps.* Buffalo, NY: Prometheus.

Oliver, J.E. (1993). Intergenerational transmission of child abuse: Rates, research, and clinical implications. *American Journal of Psychiatry*, 150, 1315-1324.

Pearson, E.S., & Hartley, H.O. (1966). *Biometrika tables for statisticians* (3 ed.). Cambridge, UK: Cambridge University Press.

Peters, J.J. (1976). Children who are victims of sexual assault and the psychology of offenders. *American Journal of Psychotherapy,* 30, 398-421.

Rada, R.T. (1976). Alcoholism and the child molester.*Annals of the New York Academy of Science,* 273, 492-496.

Russell, D. (1986). *The secret trauma: Incest in the lives of girls and women.* New York: Basic.

Seghorn, T., & Boucher, R. (1980). Sexual abuse in childhood as a factor in adult sexually dangerous criminal offenses. In J.M.Samson (Ed.), *Childhood and sexuality.* Montreal: Editions Vivantes.

Seghorn, T.K., & Boucher, R.J. (1987). Childhood sexual abuse in the lives of sexually aggressive sexual offenders.*American Journal of Child and Adolescent Psychiatry,* 26, 262-267.

Stoller, R.J. (1975). *Perversion: The erotic form of hatred.* New York: Dell.

Swift, C. (1979). The prevention of sexual child abuse: Focus on the perpetrator. *Journal of Clinical Child Psychology,* 8, 133-136.

Tingle, D., Barnard, G.W., Robins, L., Newman, G., & Hutchinson, D. (1986). Childhood and adolescent characteristics of pedophiles and rapists. *International Journal of Law and Psychiatry,* 9, 103-116.

AUTHORS' NOTES

J. Paul Fedoroff, M.D., is an assistant professor of psychiatry in the Department of Medicine, University of Toronto, and staff psychiatrist in the Forensic Division, Clarke Institute of Psychiatry. He specializes in the assessment and treatment of patients with paraphilic sexual disorders.

Shari Pinkus is completing her studies at the Osgoode Law School, York University.An earlier version of this manuscript was submitted in partial fulfillment of the requirements for an honors thesis in psychology by the second author.

Address correspondence to J. Paul Fedoroff, M.D., Forensic Division, Clarke Institute of Psychiatry, 250 College Street, Toronto, Canada M5T 1R8.

SEX OFFENDER TREATMENT
Biological Dysfunction, Intrapsychic Conflict, Interpersonal Violence. Pp. 103-123.

Assessment, Psychosexual Profiling, and Treatment of Exhibitionists

B.R. SIMON ROSSER
University of Minnesota

S. MARGRETTA DWYER
University of Minnesota

ABSTRACT Demographic and psychosexual profiles of seventy-two male exposers who presented for assessment and/or treatment at a mid-western university sexual health clinic were investigated. Associated diagnoses and treatment variables were measured. Against the stereotype of exposers as men who expose to women, 12% reported exposing to men as well. Subjects' Minnesota Multiphasic Personality Inventory scores were collated, showing exposers to have higher levels of psychopathology and sexual/gender nonconformity than other men. Indications of thought disorder and depression were also found. Mean Tennessee Self-Concept Scale scores depicted exposers as less integrated and more internally conflicted. On the Derogatis Sexual Functioning Inventory, exposers reported average sexual satisfaction but a greater number of sexually related symptoms and poorer affect. On these scales, differences were identified between single and married exposers, between court referrals and volunteers, and between those with single and multiple diagnoses. A psycho-socio-sexual construct underlying exposing behavior is proposed, with the possibility of sub-categories. *[Copies of this paper are available from The Haworth Document Delivery Service: 1-800-342-9678.]*

Exhibitionism accounts for roughly a third of all sexual offence arrests in the United States (Francoeur, 1991). There are surprisingly few studies describing the phenomenon of exhibitionism in detail, even fewer describing the population of exposers, and even less examining treatment efficacy for exhibitionism.

Most people arrested for exhibitionism are heterosexual males, although the relationship between these two demographic factors and exposing is not well understood. While isolated cases of female exhibitionism have been reported (Grob, 1985; O'Connor, 1987), in many criminal codes exhibitionism is legally defined as a male activity (Money, 1986). In several studies, exhibitionism has been associated with high levels of associated paraphilias. Lang, Langevin, Checkley, and Pugh (1987), in a comparative study of 34 male exposers and 20 non-offender controls, reported that 41% of their exposers were transvestitic, with a clear masculine gender identity. They also reported high levels of other paraphilic offending behavior, including voyeurism, telephone scatologia, frottage, toucherism, and attempted rape.

In a phallometric study of 14 exhibitionists, subjects responded to slides of fully clothed females whereas both non-exhibitionist sex offender and non-sex offender controls did not (Fedora et al., 1986). The investigators conclude that exhibitionists may respond to "nonerotic" signals in women as a consequence of cortical disinhibition.

Theories of Aetiology

Exhibitionism may be understood as a regressed or frustrated attempt at normal sexual expression, usually as the result of trauma. Money (1986) views the development of exhibitionism, like other paraphilias, as a distortion of the "lovemap," typically occurring between 5 and 8 years. According to Money, elements in courtship and sexual foreplay are displaced in the brain's norm programming and achieve abnormal importance. Once established, Money notes, the paraphilic lovemap becomes remarkably resistant to change.

Neuropsychological evidence supporting Money's theories includes links between exhibitionism and diffuse brain damage (Langevin et al., 1989, altered left hemispheric functioning (Flor et al., 1988), cortical disinhibition (Fedora, Reddon and Yeudall, 1986) and Tourette Syndrome (Comings and Comings, 1985, 1987). Freund (1988) hypothesizes that exhibitionism is symptomatic of a discrete courtship disorder; specifically, a distortion of normal pretactile interaction.

Exhibitionism has also been viewed as symptomatic of psychological distress, specifically of an underlying narcissistic personality disorder. In this model, exhibitionism represents a manifestation of internalized rage, typically by heterosexual men towards all women. In previous studies, an association between narcissism and psychological exhibitionism has been demonstrated (Raskin and Novacek, 1989; Raskin and Terry, 1988). If narcissism is related to genital exposing, then the characteristic 89/98 MMPI pattern of narcissistic personality (Raskin and Novacek, 1989) should also be present in exposers.

While the theories are not mutually exclusive, attempts have been made to test their validity. Lang et al. (1987) found in their study of exhibitionists that frequency of exhibiting was not correlated with desire for resulting intercourse. Further, while they found that nearly all the exhibitionists hoped the unsuspecting female would enjoy the experience, 20% had a history of violence-related offences. They conclude that the underlying anger together with the lack of desire for intercourse support a narcissism construct rather than Freund's courtship disorder. On the other hand, supporting his hypothesis, Freund et al. (1984) found no difference in exposers and controls on desire for intercourse.

Treatment Efficacy

Most studies of exposers over the previous ten years subsume them as part of larger studies examining efficacy of treatment of sex offenders (Dwyer and Rosser, 1992; Dwyer and Shepherd, 1990; Meyer, Cole, and Emory, 1992). Those studies providing comparative sub-analyses found interesting differences between exposers and other offenders. In studies of non-violent sex offender relapse (with and without treatment), exhibitionists have been identified as the group "most likely to reoffend" (Dwyer and Shepherd, 1990; Wiederholt, 1992). However, reviews of outcome studies report better treatment success with both child molesters and exhibitionists than with rapists (Marshall et al., 1991).

Several single case and small case studies document successful treatment for exhibitionism using psychotherapy (Lamontagne and Lesage, 1986; Perkins, 1984; Polk, 1983). More frequently, studies of psychopharmacologic agents in conjunction with cognitive/behavioral therapy report success (Murray, 1988; Perilstein et al., 1991; Rousseau et al., 1990; Wawrose and Sisto, 1992; Zbytovsky and Zapletalek, 1989). Outcome studies indicate that cognitive/behavioral programs and those using antiandrogens in conjunction with psychological treatments seem to offer the greatest hope for effectiveness and future development (Marshall et al., 1991; Marshall and Eccles, 1991).

Since most studies of exposers to date comprise small samples (less than ten), the current study was undertaken with a greater sample to examine the following five areas:

□ Demographic and social factors of exposers.

□ Psychological profiles of exposers. (Based on the theories of narcissistic personality, a 89/98 MMPI pattern of responding is predicted).

□ The sexological profile of exposers. (Based on theories of exposers as regressed and psychosexually immature or "adolescent," it is hypothesized that exposers will score significantly lower on standardized measures of sexual knowledge, sexual experience, sex role, and body image than males in the general population.)

□ Treatment efficacy for exhibitionism.

□ By comparing those respondents who successfully completed treatment, with those who ceased treatment prematurely, it is hoped to identify correlates of treatment efficacy.

METHODS

Subjects

The subject pool consisted of clients who had presented for assessment and/or treatment for exhibitionism between 1976 and 1993 at a large, out-patient sex offender program operated by the sexuality clinic of the school of medicine in a major university in the American mid-west. Included in this group were clients referred by the courts, clients who sought voluntary help and those who may have initially presented with another concern (e.g., sexual dysfunction). To be accepted into treatment, referrals from non-court referrals were required to meet DSM-III-R criteria for exhibitionism and also to have exposed on more than one occasion.

Seventy-two clients met these criteria. Of these 52 (74%) received a primary diagnosis of exhibitionism, and the remainder, a diagnosis of exhibitionism secondary to another Axis I disorder (see below). All the exposers were male, and the mean age of the sample was 30.7 years (with s.d. = 9.7, mode 26, range 13-66 years). Sixty-nine (96%) of respondents identified themselves as white Americans, with the remaining three African-American, Asian-American, and American Indian, respectively. This figure mirrors Minnesota's racial composition, estimated to be 94.4% white (Minnesota Department of Trade and Economic Development, 1992).

Apparatus

Internal clinic files were used for retrospective review of demographic factors and outcome measures. The MMPI (and MMPI-2 since 1992) was used to measure personality variables, and the Tennessee Self-Concept Scale, personality integration. The Derogatis Sexual Functioning Inventory (DSFI) was added to the assessment packet later, and thus the number of available responses was reduced.

Procedure

All charts involving sex offender assessments were reviewed, and those involving exhibitionism identified. As part of standard assessment procedures, persons presenting for sex offender treatment attend five to six one-hour interviews, and completed a battery of psychosexual testing. At the end of the assessment, each case was presented at a staff disposition meeting and associated diagnoses identified. To determine the outcome of therapy, each case was reviewed and the client's status at time of closure identified.

Demographic and Social Factors

Demographic characteristics of the 72 male exposers are detailed in Table 1. Regarding their offending, 58 (88%) of those interviewed exposed only to women, 1 (1%) exposed only to men, and 7 (11%) to both men and women. Thirty (42%) men in the sample had come to treatment via court order, while 38 (54%) were voluntary; data on the mode of referral for the remaining three could not be ascertained.

- *Table 1: Demographic Characteristics of Exposers (N = 72 Male Clinic Attendees, at Initial Assessment)*

	n	%
*Relationship Status**		
Married	36	50
Single, never married	24	33
Separated, divorced	8	11
Coupled, not married	3	4
Other	1	1
Number of Marriages		
None	25	35
One	41	58
Two	5	7
Did not answer	1	
Level of Education		
Less than high school	4	6
High school graduate	20	29
Trade school	8	11
Some college	20	29
College graduate	14	20
Graduate school	4	6
Did not answer	2	
Income		
Financially dependent	11	16
Less than 5,000	4	6
$5,000 — 15,000	9	13
$15,000 — 25,000	23	33
$25,000 — 50,000	18	26
More than $50,000	5	7

Religious Background and Current Affiliation

	Background		Current	
	n	%	n	%
Catholic	19	30	12	20
Protestant	36	57	28	47
Jewish	1	2	1	2
None	3	5	15	21
Other	4	6	5	6

* Mean length of relationship was 9.6 years; (SD = 10.14); with mode, 2 years and median, 6.5 years, ranging from 1 to 44 years.

In 65 of the 72 cases (90%), the primary presenting problem was asssessed as exhibitionism. For most exposers (45 or 63%), exhibitionism was the sole diagnosis identified at time of assessment. For the remainder, other psychiatric problems identified at time of initial assessment were mainly other sexual disorders, notably voyeurism ($n = 11$), paraphilias not otherwise specified ($n = 8$), and pedophilia ($n = 7$). Only four of 72 cases (6%) were also diagnosed as characterologically disordered. In none of these was a narcissistic personality disorder diagnosed.

Investigation of the relationship between demographic and offending factors revealed few significant differences. Of those under 28, 47% had been married at least once; of those 28 or older, over 80% had been married ($Chi^2 = 8.99$, $p < .05$). As to be expected, age, marital status, student status and income were all significantly interrelated. While 27 of 33 men who had previously received therapy at another clinic were accepted into sex offender treatment, 19 of 34 men assessed who had not been in therapy entered treatment ($Chi^2(1) = 5.23$, $p < .05$). Those who had previously been in therapy were also more likely to receive multiple diagnoses than those who had not previously been in therapy (49% vs. 24%, $Chi^2(1) = 4.53$, $p < .05$).

Psychological Profile

Table 2 profiles the Minnesota Multiphasic Personality Inventory profile for male exposers. Figure 1 profiles the Tennessee Self-Concept Scale for male exposers.

Exposers in long-term relationships scored significantly lower than single clients on TSCS total conflict ($\bar{x}_{rel} = 27.3$, $SD_{rel} = 7.3$; $\bar{x}_{sin} = 32.1$, $SD_{sin} = 8.9$; $t(61) = 2.40, p < .05$). Those court ordered to treatment scored significantly lower on the MMPI depression scale (D-2) than exposers who had entered treatment voluntarily ($\bar{x}_{crt} = 55.8$, $SD_{crt} = 19.5$, $n = 25$; $\bar{x}_{vol} = 64.6$, $SD_{vol} = 13.8$, $n = 32$; $t(55) = 2.01$, $p < .05$). There was also a trend ($p < .10$) for those court ordered to score lower on P-6 paranoia and lower on PT-7 psychasthenia scales than exposers entering treatment voluntarily. On the TSCS, those court ordered scored significantly lower on the number of deviant signs scale (NDS) than volunteers for treatment ($\bar{x}_{crt} = 6.5$, $SD_{crt} = 6.1$, $n = 2\ 7$; $\bar{x}_{vol} = 10.3$, $SD_{vol} = 6.9$, $n = 33$; $t(58) = 2.24$, $p < .05$). Not surprisingly, there were significant differences on

• *Table 2: Mean MMPI Scale Elevations for Exposers (N = 62)*

	Mean	SD	Mode	Median	Min	Max
Validity Scales						
L-scale	49.4	9.2	44	46	35	80
F-scale	59.8	11.0	58	58	46	99
K-scale	55.9	10.8	57	55	36	81
Clinical Scales						
Hypochondriasis (HS-1)	51.8	11.0	49	49	34	100
Depression (D-2)	62.6	15.2	51	63	29	106
Hysteria (HY-3)	60.5	8.8	58	60	40	80
Psychopathy (PD-4)	69.3	13.9	53	68	47	107
Masculinity-Femininity (MFF-5)	66.8	10.0	63	67	39	88
Paranoia (PA-6)	62.3	11.1	53	59	39	102
Psychanesthesia (PT-7)	60.4	14.3	54	58	38	103
Schizophrenia (PT-8)	63.9	15.7	59	61	38	119
Mania (MA-9)	58.2	12.1	52	58	32	96
Social introversion (SI-0)	53.9	10.4	54	54	36	83

the MMPI and TSCS between those given a single diagnosis and those given multiple diagnoses (see Table 3).

Sexological Profile

Figure 2 profiles the Derogatis Sexual Functioning Inventory (DSFI) for exposers ($n = 38$). Those who were court ordered to treatment recorded greater total score satisfaction than volunteers to treatment ($t(33) = 2.21, p < .05$). Those who received a single diagnosis of exposing reported significantly "healthier" scores on symptoms, affect, gender role, and overall total than those who received multiple diagnoses (see Table 4).

Treatment Efficacy

Approximately 31% (22 of 72) of exposers did not commence therapy. Almost half (34 of 72, or 48%) engaged in some therapy but left prior to graduation, 5 (7%) are currently in therapy, and 10 (14%) graduated from the sex offender program. Thus, excluding those still in treatment, of those who started therapy 10 of 44 (23%) successfully graduated.

For 65 (92%) clients, this was their first assessment at this clinic; five had been at the clinic before, and this was the third return to treatment

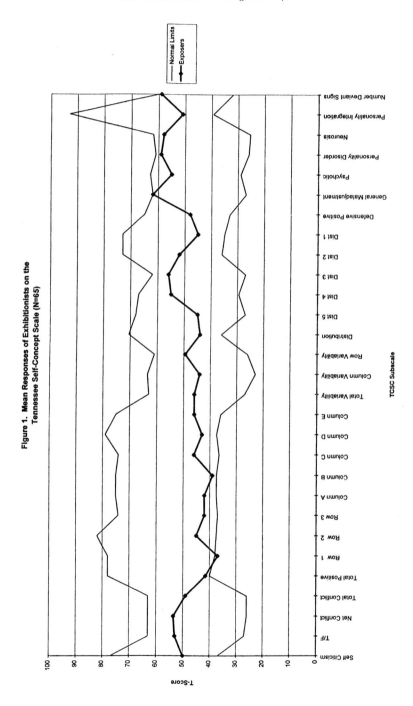

Figure 1. Mean Responses of Exhibitionists on the
Tennessee Self-Concept Scale (N=65)

- **Table 3: Diagnosis and Psychopathology in Exposers**

MMPI	Single Dx (N = 42)		Multiple Dx (N = 20)			
	Mean	SD	Mean	SD	t*	p
L	47.92	11.55	50.00	10.21	.68	
F	55.31	11.77	66.05	13.65	3.19	.005
K	55.98	13.75	52.90	10.73	.88	
HS	48.76	11.41	55.45	14.41	1.98	.05
D	58.50	15.67	68.00	18.30	2.11	.05
HY	58.69	12.44	61.30	9.98	.82	
PD	64.90	15.86	75.00	15.74	2.35	.05
MFF	64.79	13.48	67.55	12.23	.78	
PA	59.88	13.09	63.30	14.36	1.20	
PT	56.86	15.85	64.95	15.53	1.89	.06
SC	58.57	15.21	71.90	19.11	2.97	.005
MA	56.42	14.45	59.05	13.44	.68	
SI	50.38	12.62	58.30	10.36	2.43	.05
A	47.23	15.30	48.60	21.18	.29	
R	48.55	13.22	50.30	19.08	.42	
ES	53.93	14.95	44.55	18.83	2.10	.05
LB	51.36	16.47	44.21	26.89	1.25	
AL	46.97	17.36	41.05	25.04	1.05	
DY	48.95	15.85	43.84	27.02	.91	
DO	50.08	14.66	41.25	23.53	1.79	
RE	45.88	15.00	38.25	22.75	1.55	
IE	50.56	14.26	37.37	21.96	2.76	.05
ST	53.59	15.35	39.68	22.16	2.46	.05
CN	48.72	16.30	43.00	27.13	1.00	
CM	45.15	18.55	45.36	28.69	.03	

TSCS	Single Dx (N = 39		Multiple Dx (N = 26)			
	Mean	SD	Mean	SD	t**	p
Total Score	337.51	36.53	304.23	54.93	2.94	.01
Identity						
Identity	121.05	11.46	107.31	24.76	3.02	.05
Self-satisfaction	105.13	16.75	91.73	20.52	2.89	.005
Behavior	111.33	10.66	101.27	18.84	2.75	.01
Sense of Self						
Physical	69.23	12.83	63.00	12.82	1.92	.06
Moral-Ethical	65.03	10.18	58.38	12.80	2.32	.05
Personal	65.61	10.17	57.81	13.02	2.71	.01
Family	69.18	8.13	61.42	12.10	3.10	.005
Social	66.67	7.49	63.54	10.27	1.42	NS

• *Table 3 [Continued]*

Pathology Scales

Defensive Positive (DP)	55.92	11.80	46.58	16.35	2.68	.01
General Maladjustment (GM)	93.21	9.68	85.19	16.24	2.49	.05
Psychosis (PSY)	48.82	6.33	50.53	8.42	.94	
Personality Disorder (PD)	68.51	12.10	58.77	15.61	2.83	.01
Neurosis (N)	82.36	12.61	70.58	17.07	3.20	.005
Personality Integration (PI)	10.92	3.23	9.38	4.59	1.59	
Number of Deviant Signs (NDS)	7.41	6.10	11.73	8.17	2.44	.05

* $df = 60$. ** $df = 63$.

for one client. Almost half (33 of 72, or 48%) had been treated previously for exposing elsewhere.

Exposers were more likely to enter treatment during winter, than any other season. Mean stay in treatment was approximately 14 months, ranging from 1 to 68 months. During treatment, 7 clients (9.2%) were known to reoffend, 45 (63%) of clients reported they had not reoffended, and in 19 cases, reoffending was not known.

Correlates of Graduation

Taking graduation as a criterion for success in therapy, those who graduated ($n = 10$) were compared with those who entered therapy and left, but didn't graduate ($n = 33$). Non-graduates left therapy after about a year compared with two and one half years for graduates ($\bar{x}_n = 12.8$mths, $SD_n = 12.3$; $\bar{x}_g = 31.0$mths, $SD_g = 17.2$; $t(41) = 3.72, p < .001$). On the MMPI, graduates and non-graduates did not differ on the validity or clinical scales. However, on the sub-scales, non-graduates reported significantly more anxiety than graduates ($\bar{x}_n = 49.3$, $SD_n = 18.4$; $\bar{x}_g = 33.3$, $SD_g = 20.4$; $t(37) = 2.22, p < .05$). On the TSCS, non-graduates scored significantly lower on behavior ($\bar{x}_n = 104.2$, $SD_n = 17.1$; $\bar{x}_g = 113.6$, $SD_g = 9.3$; $t(29) = 2.23, p < .05$) and personality integration (PI;

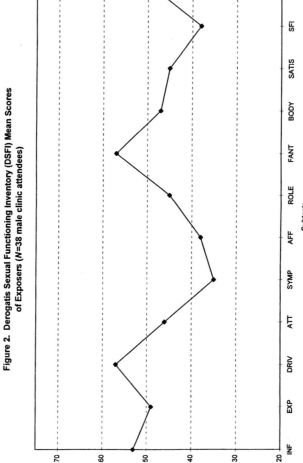

Figure 2. Derogatis Sexual Functioning Inventory (DSFI) Mean Scores of Exposers (*N*=38 male clinic attendees)

- **Table 4: Depth of Psychopathology on Sexual Functioning in Exposers**

DSFI	Single Dx (N = 24)		Multiple Dx (N = 14)			
	Mean	SD	Mean	SD	t*	p
Information	50.25	12.10	44.79	11.20	1.38	
Experience	48.42	11.42	50.14	11.10	.46	
Drive	53.21	9.36	57.57	7.93	1.47	
Attitudes	42.88	10.71	45.21	7.51	0.72	
Symptoms	41.17	10.24	31.21	7.57	3.16	.005
Affect	43.12	12.27	32.39	11.01	2.72	.01
Gender role	47.50	6.98	37.00	8.72	4.08	.001
Fantasy	52.00	14.77	53.86	12.79	0.39	
Body image	42.88	7.72	38.93	8.18	1.49	
Satisfaction	49.04	6.55	44.29	9.42	1.83	.075
Sexual Functioning	42.33	14.22	33.00	8.96	2.21	.05
Subjective Sexual Functioning	51.29	11.62	48.84	12.71	.59	

* $df = 36$

$\bar{x}_n = 9.9$, $SD_n = 3.8$; $\bar{x}_g = 13.3$, $SD_g = 3.2$; $t(40) = 2.54$, $p < .05$), and higher on number of deviant signs (NDS: $\bar{x}_n = 10.8$, $SD_n = 7.6$; $\bar{x}_g = 4.13$, $SD_g = 6.0$; $t(40) = 2.54$, $p < .05$).

On the DSFI, non-graduates reported lower scores on sexual experience ($\bar{x}_n = 49.8$, $SD_n = 12.5$; $\bar{x}_g = 56.6$, $SD_g = 3.6$; $t(22) = 2.06$, $p < .05$), fantasy ($\bar{x}_n = 52.6$, $SD_n = 14.4$; $\bar{x}_g = 67.2$, $SD_g = 10.0$; $t(22) = 2.12$, $p < .05$), and overall sexual functioning (SFI: $_n = 37.8$, $SD_n = 12.8$; $\bar{x}_g = 54.6$, $SD_g = 10.1$; $t(22) = 2.71$, $p < .01$).

DISCUSSION

The usual caveats applying to sex offender research are applicable to this study. It is to be remembered that this study is of exposers who were caught and those who volunteered for treatment. It is not known how these factors might differentiate the sample from the larger population of exhibitionists. Also, while data was collected using standardized techniques, over seventeen years, some behavioral drift in interviewing techniques cannot be excluded. Also, rationalization and distortion on the part of the exposer may have influenced the results.

The purpose of profiling needs to be addressed. The psychometrics of profiling assumes that there is a distinct psychological pattern across the population of exposers. However, mean scores across many measures may mask multiple patterns of responding. Ideally, cluster analysis would clarify this possibility. Unfortunately, the sample, while large by comparison with other studies was too small to validly undertake this procedure. Thus, the profile summaries herein should be taken as indicative of common problems encountered in treating exhibitionists, rather than definitive of the population of exhibitionists. It is within these limitations that the above results are discussed.

Demographic and Social Factors

Most exposers presenting for treatment appear to be young (less than 30 years), had exposed to women, and were married or in a long-term relationship. Most appear well-educated with over half having received some college education and a quarter having graduated. Congruent with the education findings, most exposers report average to above average income. And most were voluntary referrals to treatment.

While the phenomenon of exhibitionism as being predominantly a disorder of young heterosexual males is not surprising, other demographic factors in the results deserve further discussion. The above average education and income level for the sample counters clinical impressions of exposers as self-defeating, but may just be a screening bias. The cost of engaging in therapy at the medical school sexuality clinic would bias the study towards those with insurance and those on higher incomes.

Three of these findings deserve further consideration. First, against stereotype, most exposers were married at time of assessment. Only one third were single, never married. Second, against previous findings that present exposing as a disorder against women, approximately 12% of the sample reported "bisexual" exposing. (Except for the one person who exposed exclusively to men, it is not known if these men were deliberately exposed to, or viewed by the exposer as merely incidental to their desire to expose to women.) Third, most exposers presented voluntarily for treatment, suggesting that even without legal pressure, most exposers in treatment perceive their behavior as problematic.

Some of the findings appear intriguing. Surprisingly, those court ordered to treatment did not differ from those seeking treatment voluntarily on demographic factors such as age, educational level, income, or marital status.

For over half of the clients presenting for treatment, exposing was diagnosed the only significant issue. For the remainder, exposing was associated with other paraphilias and in a small minority, other psychopathology. Against Raskin and Novacek's hypothesis of exhibitionism as symptomatic of a narcissistic personality disorder, only a minority of exposers were diagnosed with non-sexually related psychiatric diagnoses, and none with narcissistic personality disorder.

Psychological Factors

Examination of the mean MMPI responses provides mixed support for a psychopathogical construct underlying exhibitionism. While the 89/98 profile predicted by Raskin and Novacek's (1989) hypothesis clearly was not found, an elevated 45(8) profile was demonstrated. This profile matches clinical impressions of exhibitionists. According to Graham (1990, 97-98),

> Persons with the 45/54 code tend to be rather immature and narcissistic. They are emotionally passive, and they harbor very strong unrecognized dependency needs. They have difficulty incorporating societal values into their own personalities. They are nonconforming, and they seem to be defying convention through their dress, speech, and behavior . . . a low frustration tolerance, coupled with intense feelings of anger and resentment, can lead to brief periods of aggressive acting out. Temporary remorse and guilt may follow the acting out behavior, but 45/54 persons are not likely to be able to inhibit similar episodes in the future. The modal diagnosis for psychiatric patients with the 45/54 code is passive-aggressive personality disorder. Persons with the 45/54 code are likely to be experiencing difficulty with sex role identity. They are rebelling against stereotyped sex roles. Males with the 45/54 code fear being dominated by females, and they are extremely sensitive to demands of females.

While Graham notes a link between an elevated 45/54 profile and overt homosexuality, the description of a 45/54 personality better fits the exhibitionist. The mean Sc-8 score of 63.9 is consistent with disturbances of thinking, mood and behavior, including extremely poor judgement,

• *Table 5: Responses of Exposers (N = 56) on Selected MMPI Sub-scales*

Sub-scale	Mean	SD	Mode	Median	Min	Max
A	51.1	12.0	42	46	35	80
R	52.6	7.9	47	53	38	78
ES	54.4	10.1	59	56	24	72
LB	54.7	12.5	62	57	28	83
AL	50.2	13.7	37	49	26	79
DY	52.7	12.6	61	52	31	83
DO	53.4	9.8	53	53	28	70
RE	48.1	11.4	47	49	21	71
IE	51.6	9.2	52	54	28	67
ST	54.7	9.0	53	55	33	75
CN	52.3	13.3	50	50	17	79
CM	52.5	13.5	37	49	34	91

social isolation, shyness, apprehension, internal hostility, feelings of inferiority, immaturity and lack of basic problem-solving strategies (Graham, 1990). Prognosis for psychotherapy is poor. A mean D-2 score of 62.6 may help explain why some exhibitionists report relief from antidepressants (Fedoroff, 1992). Mean responses of subjects in this study on selected sub-scales of the MMPI are reported in Table 5.

The implications for treatment include the need to see exhibitionism as symptomatic of developmental delay. As well as cognitive-behavioral therapy aimed at teaching socio-sexual skills, greater attention to internalized feelings of self-doubt, hostility, dependency and sex role conflict are warranted.

While most of the Tennessee Self-Concept Scale (TSCS) means were (just) within normal limits, the overall profile is consistent with the image of exposers as poorly integrated and conflicted. In particular, issues of basic self-identity and moral-ethical worth appear pertinent to explore in cases of exhibitionism.

Those in relationship reported significantly lower levels of self-esteem than single exhibitionists. This is consistent with reports by exposers in relationships of feeling intimidated, beaten down, dominated and controlled. Treating exhibitionism systemically, rather than solely as an intrapsychic acting out, appears important. Thus, couple's therapy is indicated for those exposers in relationship. It also suggests that encouraging exposers to have relationships prematurely may paradoxically increase the degree of pathology involved.

Those court ordered appear less depressed and better adjusted on the MMPI and TSCS scales than those voluntarily seeking treatment. A number of reasons could account for this. Those court ordered may feel relief at being sentenced, satisfaction at having been caught, or less responsibility when the decision to enter treatment is taken out of their control.

The differentiation between those with single diagnoses and those with multiple diagnoses was supported by the significant differences found on many of the MMPI and almost all of the TSCS scales (see Table 3). This would indicate that assessment of exposers should include some assessment of comorbidity or depth of associated psychopathology. It further raises the possibility of exhibitionism being a disorder of multiple aetiologies; for some being a simple courtship disorder, or for others being a complex acting out of underlying psychopathology.

Sexological Factors

Examination of the DSFI scores indicates that, against the stereotype of exposers as having poor sex lives, overall satisfaction of the sample was average. On both symptoms and affect, exposers scored significantly lower than the normative sample, possibly reflecting the extreme sensitivity to sexual situations and negative affect noted above. Scores on the DSFI indicate that most exhibitionists report average knowledge about sex and about "normal" sex drives and interest in sex.

Because of the small numbers involved, the differences between those court ordered and volunteers on sexual functioning measures should be taken as suggestive only. Nevertheless, like the psychological profiles, the sexological profile indicates those court ordered to be a more satisfied and sexually healthier sample than voluntary clients. Not surprisingly those with multiple diagnoses reported poorer scores on many of the sexological questionnaires.

Taken together, the psychological and sexological profiles would seem to indicate a psycho-socio-sexual construct underlying exposing behavior. In developmental terms, the average exposer does appear

regressed and preoccupied with "adolescent" concerns re: self acceptance, sexual identity, and internalized hostility.

Treatment Efficacy

Only 23% of exposers in treatment graduated. In addition, as Dwyer
(1988) reported, treated exposers have the highest recidivism rate of
treated non-violent sex offenders. Clearly, the prognosis is poor for
someone entering treatment, although while in treatment, the likelihood
of re-exposing appears low. Clearly more research into treatment techniques and barriers to graduation is in order. The findings support clinical
observations that many exposers leave just prior to program completion.
Greater assistance to the exhibitionist preparing to graduate may be
indicated.

The differences between graduates and non-graduates may yield some
insight into why exhibitionists have so much difficulty finishing therapy.
While the mean difference in months in therapy must reflect some degree
of drop-out across the therapy process, non-graduates appeared more
anxious, less functional, less integrated, and more "deviant" in other
behaviors at initial assessment. Thus, within the population of exposers,
there appears a subgroup of exposers who are more isolated, less healthy,
more sexually shut down and less amenable to treatment.

While some promising work is being conducted into the effects of
neuromodulating medications on exhibitionism, a comprehensive strat-
egy to treating exposers would include such factors as medication to
assist the exposer gain control over the behavior, teaching of sociosexual
skills, promotion of developmental maturation, exploration of intrapsychic distress, and group therapy to limit isolation, provide peer support
and promote intimacy. Each of these factors would appear important to
the successful treatment of exhibitionism. More research investigating
those factors that distinguish exposers who successfully complete therapy from those who enter but drop out would appear warranted. And new
studies incorporating advances in both psychopharmacology and psychotherapy on the treatment and recidivism of exposers would appear the
next step in coming to a truly scientific appreciation of the mechanisms
underlying exhibitionism.

REFERENCES

American Psychiatric Association, (1987). *Diagnostic and Statistical Manual of Mental Disorders, Third Edition, Revised* (DSM-III-R). Washington, DC: American Psychiatric Association.

Comings, D.E. and Comings, B.G. (1985). Tourette syndrome: clinical and psychological aspects of 250 cases. *American Journal of Human Genetics,* 37(3):435-450.

Comings, D.E. and Comings, B.G. (1987). A controlled study of Tourette syndrome. IV. Obsessions, compulsions, and schizoid behaviors. *American Journal of Human Genetics,* 41(5):782-803.

Dwyer, S.M. (1988). Exhibitionism/voyeurism. *Journal of Social Work and Human Sexuality,* 7(1):101-102.

Dwyer, S.M. and Myers, S. (1990). Sex offender treatment: a six-month to ten-year follow-up study. *Annals of Sex Research,* 3(3):305-318.

Dwyer,S.M. and Rosser, B.R.S. (1992). Treatment outcome research: Cross-referencing a six-month to ten-year follow-up study on sex offenders. *Annals of Sex Research,* 5:87-97.

Erickson, W.D., Walbek, N.H. & Seely, R.K. Behavior patterns of child mollesters. *Archives of Sexual Behavior,* 17(1):77-86

Fedoroff, P., (1992, October). Disease, behavior and paraphilias: a preliminary study. National Conference on Sexual Compulsivity/Addiction, Minneapolis, MN.

Fedora, O., Reddon, J.R., and Yeudall, L.T. (1986). Stimuli eliciting sexual arousal in genital exhibitionists: a possible clinical application. *Archives of Sexual Behavior,* 15(5):417-427.

Flor, H.P., Lang, R.A., Koles, Z.J., and Frenzel, R.R. (1988). Quantitative EEG investigation of genital exhibitionism. *Annals of Sex Research,* 1(1):49-62.

Francoeur, R.T. (1991). *Becoming a Sexual Person.* New York: Macmillan.

Freund, K. (1988) Courtship disorder: Is this hypothesis valid? *Annals of the New York Academy of Sciences,* 528:172-182.

Freund, K., Scher, H., and Hucker, S. (1984). The courtship disorders: a further investigation. *Archives of Sexual Behavior,* 13(2):133-139.

Graham, J.R. (1990). *MMPI-2: Assessing Personality and Psychopathology.* New York: Oxford University Press.

Grob, C.S. (1985). Female Exhibitionism. *Journal of Nervous and Mental Disease,* 173(4):253-256.

Green, D., (1987). Adolescent exhibitionists: theory and therapy. *Journal of Adolescence,* 10:45-56.

Lang, R.A., Langevin, R., Checkley, K.L., and Pugh, G. (1987). Genital exhibitionism: Courtship disorder or narcissism? *Canadian Journal of Behavioral Science,* 19(2):216-232.

122 SEX OFFENDER TREATMENT

Langevin, R., Lang, R.A., Wortzman, G., Frenzel, R.R. et al., (1989). An examination of brain damage and dysfunction in genital exhibitionists. *Annals of Sex Research*, 2(1):77-87.

Kinsey, A.C., Pomeroy, W.B., and Martin, C.E. (1948). *Sexual Behavior in the Human Male*. Philadelphia: W.B. Saunders.

Lamontagne, Y. & Lesage, A. (1986) Private exposure and covert sensitization in the treatment of exhibitionism. *Journal of Behavior Therapy and Experimental Psychiatry*, 17(3):197-201.

Marshall, W.L. & Eccles, A. (1991). Issues in clinical practice with sex offenders. *Journal of Interpersonal Violence*, 6(1):68-93.

Minnesota Department of Trade and Economic Development: Business Development and Analysis Division, 1992. *Compare Minnesota: An Economic and Statistical Fact Book 1992-93*. Minnesota Department of Trade and Economic Development: St. Paul.

Marshall, W.L. & Eccles, A. (1991) Issues in clinical practice with sex offenders. *Journal of Interpersonal Violence*, 6(1), 68-83.

Marshall, W.L., Jones, R., Ward, T., Johnson, P. et al. (1991). Treatment outcome with sex offenders. *Clinical Psychology Review*, 11(4):465-485.

Money, J. (1986). *Lovemaps: Clinical Concepts of Sexual-Erotic Health and Pathology, Paraphilia, and Gender Transposition in Childhood, Adolescence, and Maturity*. New York: Irvington.

Murray, J.B. (1988). Psychopharmacological therapy of deviant sexual behavior. *Journal of General Psychology*, 115(1):101-110.

Meyer, W.J., Cole, C., and Emory, E. (1992) Depo provera treatment for sex offending behavior: an evaluation of outcome. *Bulletin of the American Academy of Psychiatry and the Law*, 20(3):249-59.

Myers, R.G., and Berah, E.F. (1983). Some features of Australian exhibitionists compared with pedophiles. *Archives of Sexual Behavior*, 12(6):541-547.

Perkins, D. (1984) Psychological treatment of offenders in prison and the community. *Issues in Criminology and Legal Psychology*, 6:36-46.

O'Connor, A. (1987). Female sex offenders. *British Journal of Psychiatry*, 150:615-620.

Perilstein, R.D., Lipper, S., & Friedman, L.J. (1991). Three cases of parapahilias responsive to fluoxetine treatment. *Journal of Clinical Psychiatry*, 52(4):169-170.

Raskin, R., and Novacek, J. An MMPI description of the narcissistic personality. *Journal of Personality Assessment*, 53(1):66-80.

Raskin, R. and Terry, H. (1988). A principal components analysis of the Narcissistic Personality Inventory and further evidence of its construct validity. *Journal of Personality and Social Psychology*, 54(5), 890-902.

Roid, G.H., and Fitts, W.H. (1988). *Tennessee Self-Concept Scale (TSCS)*. Los Angeles: Western Psychological Services.

Rousseau, L., Couture, M., Dupont, A., Labrie, F., & Couture, N. (1990). Effect of combined androngen blockade with an LHRH agonist and flutamide in one severe case of exhibitionism. *Canadian Journal of Psychiatry,* 35(4):338-341.

Saunders, E., Awad, G.A., and White, G. (1986). Male adolescent sex offenders: the offender and the offences. *Canadian Journal of Psychiatry,* 31(6):542-9.

U.S. Bureau of the Census, 1992. *Statistical Abstract of the United States: 1992* (112th edition). Washington, D.C., 1992.

Walrose, F.E., & Sisto, T.M. (1992). Cloripramine and a case of exhibitionism. *American Journal of Psychiatry,* 149(6):843.

Wiederholt, I.C. The psychodynamics of sex offenses and implications for treatment. *Journal of Offender Rehabilitation,* 18(3-4):19-24.

Zbytovsky, J., & Zapletalek, M. (1989) Haloperidol decanoate in the treatment of sexual deviations. *Activitas Nervosa Superior,* 31(1):41-42.

AUTHORS' NOTES

B.R. Simon Rosser, PhD, is a licensed psychologist and assistant professor in the Program in Human Sexuality, Department of Family Practice and Community Health, Medical School, University of Minnesota.

S. Margretta Dwyer, MA, LP, is coordinator of the sex offender treatment program at the Program in Human Sexuality, Department of Family Practice and Community Health, Medical School, University of Minnesota.

The authors wish to acknowledge the staff and clients of the sex offender program at the Program in Human Sexuality, for their assistance in recruitment, treatment and data collection. Deb Finstad and Karen Scheltma provided computer assistance for this report.

Address correspondence to Dr. B.R. Simon Rosser, 1300 South Second Street, Suite 180, Minneapolis, MN 55454.

SEX OFFENDER TREATMENT
Biological Dysfunction, Intrapsychic Conflict, Interpersonal Violence. Pp. 125-141.

Treatment Successes with Mentally Retarded Sex Offenders

DAVID NOLLEY
Cupertino, California

LYNNE MUCCIGROSSO
Stiggall & Associates, Los Gatos, California

ERIC ZIGMAN
Skills Center, Inc., Santa Cruz, California

ABSTRACT Eight men with mental retardation, residing in the community, were enrolled in treatment that extended across home and their work place. All the men had been referred for services through their case management agency because of culturally unacceptable expressive sexual behaviors and five of them had been jailed for alleged sex offenses, mostly for Child Molestation. After three years, the major product of treatment was that there were no other sex offenses committed. As a result, all the men remained outside of institutional confinement subsequent to beginning treatment. Collateral, positive benefits of treatment also included: successes in cultur-ally-normative relationship formation, improvements in their adaptive skills useful in the community and at work/day program, movement to less restric-tive living environment, and successful treatment of other DSM-III-R diag-noses. Treatment elements consisted of: individual therapy and individual education in sexuality, culturally appropriate social skills, and assertiveness; Group Therapy that combined education and therapy; coordination therapy and educational services with family or care providers through in-home services and on-site consultation with Day Program/Vocational Training agency staff. All the educational and therapeutic tools and devices used were easily available from commercial sources. *[Copies of this paper are available from The Haworth Document Delivery Service: 1-800-342-9678.]*

As Senn (1988) has noted, there is a speculative professional literature that depicts persons with mental retardation as sexually dangerous. Gebhard (1977) has made the statement that "Consent cannot legally be given (for sex) by individuals who are mentally defective." There is also a common myth about mentally retarded men with as being "over-sexed" and thus potential sex offenders (Hall, 1974). These fallacies have been used to institutionalize persons with mental and sexual problems (Adams, Tallorn & Alcorn, 1982). It is also incorrect to substitute these faulty impressions with unscientific conceptions of persons with mental retardation as being without sexuality. Without data, it is correct to say that it is not known if persons with mental retardation differ from others in regard to deviant sexuality.

Gebhard (1977) estimated, without reference to a source, that persons with mental retardation or brain damage constitute 10%-15% of identified offenders, and their offenses consisted mostly of child molestation, exhibitionism, and voyeurism ("peeping"). In contrast, Swanson and Garwick (1990) showed that only 3% of citizens with mental retardation in the metropolitan area they served had been identified to have committed sex offenses.

Treatment programs directed to persons with mental retardation began to appear only during the past two decades. Most treatment programs are located within locked, institutional or residential settings (Haaven, Little & Petre-Miller, 1987; Losada-Paisey & Paisey, 1988; Nolley, 1975; 1978), but some programs treat persons in the community (Demetral, 1989; Griffiths, Quinsey & Hingsburger, 1989).

Swanson and Garwick (1990) reported that their population of "low functioning sex offenders" were commonly ignored or only scolded, rather than introduced to therapy or training. However, persons with mental retardation, who are charged with criminal sexual conduct, are usually remanded to a facility for individuals with mental retardation rather than undergo legal proceedings, as citizens without a diagnosis of mental retardation must (Monat-Haller, 1992). According to Swanson and Garwick, "these sex offenders are typically desensitized gradually to the gravity of the offenses and then unexpectedly punished." Monat-Haller further indicated that sex offender treatment services to persons suspected of mental retardation were usually reserved for those with IQs of 80 or above, on the common presumption that only those who can understand psychological processes (such as those involved in group therapy) that are "cognitive and abstract" can benefit from these services. If this is true, then persons with mental retardation, whose cognitive level may be in the tested moderate or mild range, are at a considerable disadvantage. That is, they may not be prosecuted for a crime but, instead, be remanded for custody to a public facility where, in turn, they may languish without appropriate therapy and training that could otherwise render them fit for success in community placement. Such a "sentence" might be indeterminate and could then be life-long.

According to Monat-Haller (1992, p. 178), "group process is preferred in dealing with sexual offenses" among retarded offenders, as it is the standard in therapy programs for nonhandicapped persons (cf., Dwyer & Meyers, 1990). Monat-Haller continued (pp. 179-181):

> Groups that are developed to work with sex offenders with mental retardation do better if they are run by two therapists . . . [these groups] . . . should meet weekly [and] can vary in size from four to ten members . . . the average length of stay in a group for sex offenders with mental retardation . . . is two to two and a half years . . .

Similar to work with adolescent sex offenders, plethysmography is rarely used with alleged sex offenders who are mentally retarded (Lund, 1992; Monat-Haller, 1992).

Demetral (1989) offered comprehensive services to men with mental retardation who were enrolled in treatment for sex offenses. He reported a recidivism rate of less than 2%, which is substantially below that reported for nonhandicapped adults (Dwyer & Meyers, 1990). However, like most other published treatment programs that appeared during the past 15 years, there has been insufficient time since treatment to conduct long term follow up. In contrast, Haaven et al. (1990) reported a recidivism rate of 23% for sexual offenses among their mentally retarded subjects.

Many adults diagnosed with mental retardation have been sheltered from learning opportunities such that their awareness of the responsibilities of adult citizenship has been blunted. Our experience, like that of others who deal with the sexual concerns of persons with mental retardation (e.g., Monat-Haller, 1992; Swanson & Garwick, 1990) is that clients who are chronologically adult but suffer mental retardation often have naive ideas about sexuality; such ideas may be closer to children's or adolescents' ideas of sexuality. This report will describe our analysis of the culturally unacceptable sexual behavior of a sample of adult men with mental retardation and, based upon that analysis, the development of remedial treatment that produced *zero* recidivism after cessation of alleged sex offenses for up to three years after treatment began.

METHOD

Referral for Services

The subjects were referred from a local case management agency, for individualized sex education and counseling in an effort to correct various sexual behavior problems. Together with judgements by vocational training staff, these sources agreed about who should receive treatment. Pertinent characteristics of subjects are displayed in Table 1.

Group Education

Lesson plans were devised, based on what was known of the subjects, to eliminate further criminal sexual behavior. The group began with get-acquainted and self esteem building activities. Subjects and facilitators together established ground rules for making the group safe and manageable. The group developed a list of what they wanted to know more about, related to sexuality. Beginning the group in this way was intended to enhance subjects' self esteem and feelings of empowerment, and build a sense of ownership, or buy-in, to the group (Muccigrosso, Scavarda, Simpson-Brown & Thallacker, 1991).

The educator's "lesson plan" must be flexible. Educational strategies often prompted clinical opportunities which often took priority for the group's attention. In a sense, the education led to the "therapeutic moments." Over time, the sessions tended to move from more formal educational presentation to less structured group discussion. However, the facilitators sought to keep the focus on essential treatment goals of

- *Table 1: Characteristics of Offenders, Including Age, Functional Level,
  Sexual Issues Precipitating Treatment, Other Relevant Diagnoses, and
  Arraignment/Incarceration History*

Subject	1 [Age = 20]
Functional Level	Moderate
Sexual Issue[s]	Child molestation
Other Diagnosis[es]	None
Arraigned/Imprisoned?	Yes
Subject	2 [Age = 40]
Functional Level	Mild
Sexual Issue[s]	Child molestation
Other Diagnosis[es]	Pedophilia
Arraigned/Imprisoned?	No
Subject	3 [Age = 29]
Functional Level	Mild
Sexual Issue[s]	Child molestation
Other Diagnosis[es]	Cerebral palsy
Arraigned/Imprisoned?	No
Subject	4 [Age = 20]
Functional Level	Borderline
Sexual Issue[s]	Child molestation, penile injury
Other Diagnosis[es]	Social phobia
Arraigned/Imprisoned?	Yes
Subject	5 [Age = 19]
Functional Level	Mild
Sexual Issue[s]	Child molestation
Other Diagnosis[es]	Post-traumatic stress disorder
Arraigned/Imprisoned?	Yes
Subject	6 [Age = 25]
Functional Level	Mild
Sexual Issue[s]	Child molestation
Other Diagnosis[es]	Pedophilia
Arraigned/Imprisoned?	Yes
Subject	7 [Age = 23]
Functional Level	Borderline
Sexual Issue[s]	Child molestation
Other Diagnosis[es]	Williams syndrome
Arraigned/Imprisoned?	Yes
Subject	8 [Age = 36]
Functional Level	Mild
Sexual Issue[s]	Child molestation
Other Diagnosis[es]	None
Arraigned/Imprisoned?	Yes

no reoffenses and the development of culturally normative replacement behavior for staying "safe" from reoffense.

It is important to realize that therapy and education for identified sex offenders cannot be satisfied by a short range project. There is not a "quick fix." Funding authorities, facilitators, families and care providers must understand beforehand that a commitment to a minimum of two years therapy is likely and that maintenance of no reoffenses is the only useful measure of the quality of service delivery rather than the delivery of *x* sessions of interventions.

Specific Group Teaching Strategies

We found that participation was superior to lectures, to draw out participation from subjects rather than to attempt to pump information in as though it is a variation of a classroom. This can be done through role play and practice of the skills being taught (Korinek & Polloway, 1993) and games, like board games, that help to teach to the objectives. Repetition is critical; more experienced group members can solidify their learnings by assisting in repetitive presentations of material to their peers. Facilitators must be concrete and explicit. Therefore, it is useful to work on learning of a common vocabulary (e.g., "consent," "illegal"). Get feedback from members to ascertain the strength of learning of culturally acceptable behaviors (Kempton, 1993; Muccigrosso, 1991).

The "Four Ps"

To make simple and memorable the rules about sexual expression, the facilitators taught these rules for sexual expression (see Prendergast, 1991):

❑ Privacy — sexual expression only in private.

❑ Permission — sexual expression only with persons who agree and are able to agree.

❑ Protection — all genital sexual expression with another person requires condom use.

❑ Partner over the age of 18 — sex only with an adult; NO CHILDREN, even if the child says, or appears to say, "yes.".

Relationship Development

Society's ignorance regarding the human relationship needs of persons with developmental disabilities is part of the historical explanation for the lack of educational models for relationship skills development. Relationship skills have been largely ignored (Hingsburger, 1989). Persons with developmental disabilities may be seeking sexual gratification without regard to any standards. In other words, if it is never acceptable to be sexual (as among so many people with developmental disabilities), then what solutions are there but to go ahead, reach out and experiment (Hingsburger, Griffiths & Quinsey, 1991)? Since these subjects had already shown a willingness to "experiment," we felt that assisting them to develop relationship formation skills was essential. Discussion and work in the group focussed on positive relationship development to replace criminal sexual expression.

Assessment

Guidelines for assessment were provided by Greer and Stuart (1983), Leyin and Dicks (1987) and Lund (1992). Sources of arousal were identified by self-report and clinical interview during individual sessions with the licensed psychologist facilitator. However, as this source is widely viewed to be unreliable (Weinrott & Saylor, 1988), information was also sought from the case management agency files, significant others, and Police reports. There was questionable agreement across sources of clinical history. For example, parents sometimes deny that their adult, mentally disabled offspring have sexual feelings (Monat-Haller, 1992), while group home staff see sexual indiscretions daily. Sources for "clinical assessment" included:

- ❑ Periodic interviews with parents, siblings, and other family, professional group home supervisors, vocational training supervisors, and independent living skills trainers.

- ❑ Direct observation and products of personal interview during sessions.

- ❑ Direct observation and products of personal interview at home.

Penile recordings were not used with these subjects from a protected population, in which integrity of consent may be questionable (Lund, 1992). Social skills deficits were assessed through self-reports and role-playing exercises custom developed for these subjects. Knowledge of culturally acceptable sexual behavior was assessed by published inventories and through clinical interviews. Structured assessment included past intellectual assessments and adaptive behavioral inventories that had been used to establish or verify mental disability.

Structured assessments of sexual history and behavior were not done at the outset because we hypothesized, in agreement with Leyin and Dicks (1983) and Dwyer and Rosser (1992), that subjects might fabricate answers to intrusive questions early in education/treatment. Also, we thought that intrusive questioning might hinder start-up of group process because it would interfere with rapport-building. Subsequent examination of this hypothesis strengthened our belief in its integrity. To illustrate: Whereas only one group member admitted to his offense during session one (he had already been in individual therapy for his disorder for several years), there were still two group members who would not acknowledge their offenses, four months after treatment began. Both subjects eventually acknowledged their offenses; only then did their structured assessment occur. Structured assessment began when the facilitators agreed that there was sufficient trust among the group members and the facilitators that there would be honesty in responding.

Assessment tools were chosen based upon our subjective judgements about their face validity, unique content, relevance, clarity of item description, appropriateness to the developmental level of the group members, and low intrusiveness. The assessment tools had not undergone scientific studies to establish reliability and/or validity and we are not aware of any means to assess sexuality in persons with mental handicaps that have been subjected to such studies. The structured assessments, the Life Facts: Sexuality Questionnaire (Stanfield, 1990) and the Woodvale Sexuality Assessment (Woodvale Management Services, 1989) were completed through direct interview.

Individual Diagnosis and Clinical Behavior Therapy

Each subject was given a Mental Status Examination (MSE) prior to group services by the clinician facilitator. Together with history and background furnished by the case management agency, the MSE was used to screen for disorders that might impact service delivery. In addition to diagnoses summarized in Table 1, the MSE discovered a sociopathic disorder in a subject who was returned to a secure (locked) state facility by court order after repeated offenses during the pre-treatment evaluation period. Another man's schizophrenia was confirmed, and he was also excluded from the group while efforts were made to stabilize him on medication.

Diagnostic services were also used to clarify any influences Axis III diagnoses might have on service delivery. For example, the cognitive limitations of one man with an Axis III diagnosis of Williams Syndrome was useful to personalize his therapy.

Clinical behavioral services were delivered both in individual and in group sessions. For example, we hypothesized that self control of behavior in one domain might facilitate self control of other sorts of behavior. Therefore, one aim of individual and group therapy was to control anger, a behavior as easy to measure as sex offense but of much higher rate, to help inhibit sex offending impulses. To accomplish this goal, role play of anger resolution strategies and anger control exercises were used and the efficacy of this therapy was subsequently measured by observing subjects' anger about comparatively trivial matters.

Several of the men were group home residents and they brought problems from this source to the group for solution, intermixed with their problems of culturally acceptable expressive sexuality. Cognitive behavioral techniques of modeling problem-solving strategies and stress reduction techniques, including relaxation, were useful in helping these men express themselves more clearly.

Small Group Process

Highly structured sessions were used to focus attention and teach effective group interaction techniques (listening, talking in turn, etc.). Even in early, process-building sessions, some time was left each week to deal with participants' individual issues, especially if they related to sexuality. As group participants came to understand group interaction skills and the value and purpose of group therapy, less structured sessions would occasionally occur (Pfadt, 1991). Either individual issues would arise in a participant's daily life or educational materials would "spark" a discussion of past experiences. In these cases the clinician facilitator would usually guide the discussions to try and provide a therapeutic context in which the participant could explore his feelings and behavior around a specific issue. For example, a participant might see a picture of a policeman arresting someone for illegal sexual expression and this might act as a catalyst for a participant's disclosure of his arrest experience.

By the end of the first year, much of the basic, essential educational components had been presented and discussed. Rehearsing the material, or presenting it to new participants, afforded opportunities to both reinforce previous learning and test effectiveness of previous presentations. When a participant brought an issue into the group which presented the opportunity to either explore past mistakes or build strategies to avoid possible future mistakes, the facilitators tried to make effective use of the issue for the entire group even if it meant "shelving" the session's educational plan for that meeting.

It should be noted that introduction of new members to the group, once this deeper level of emotional processing was reached, tended to return the group to the "rapport-building" stage of earlier meetings. Highly structured educational materials again offered a reliable way of returning group focus to the essential issues and rebuilding the levels of inter-member empathy and trust.

Because all participants originally were employed at the same sheltered workshop facility, a direct service supervisor was enlisted to co-facilitate the group. This "program facilitator" acted as both liaison to and monitor of the participants as they moved through their work day. Experienced residential or vocational direct-service staff make ideal candidates for this role. It is essential that the issues of the daily lives of the participants be brought into group and that the work of the group be carried over into the daily lives of the participants.

The educator directed the planning of educational objectives, obtained or developed materials and strategies for teaching, delivered the "lesson," and directed the group members in this process. As responses began to be forthcoming from the group members, all three facilitators participated.

Group Process and Culturally-Normative Relationship Skills

Besides the primary outcome, many benefits of treatment became apparent. Some of these were results of group participation and group process. Participants became better able to listen to other members and help them work through feelings or suggest strategies to overcome present obstacles. Sharing of similar feelings (e.g., guilt, frustration, sexual need) was the basis for both the formation of inter-group friendships and acquisition of relationship-building skills as well as reduction of some participants' feelings of isolation and hopelessness.

Facilitation of problem-solving strategies became a powerful component of group process, allowing participants to work on plans of action which could alter the conditions of their lives. Reduced egocentrism was also seen in many of the participants as a result of treatment. The group offered not only a forum for the individual issues raised by members to be discussed, but also shaped their ability to assist others in exploring issues and problems. This peer training increased as group cohesion developed and resulted in higher self-esteem and a more developed sense of empathy in the participants.

Socialization is not seen as a need or goal in most homes where our subjects resided. Not many of our subjects had been encouraged, supported or even allowed to date or work toward independent (or semi-independent) social opportunities.

RESULTS OF ASSESSMENT

Assessment of knowledge acquisition was contaminated by level of cognitive functioning. Moderately mentally handicapped subjects scored lowest on these assessments (average score 109 out of 200 total) while the subjects who tested within Borderline Normal IQ scored highest (162/200) on these assessments. This trend was evident across all four domains of knowledge surveyed: Basic Biological Knowledge, Culturally-acceptable Sexual Behavior, Health Practices, and Relationships. We hypothesized that subjects' receptive impairments may have impaired their acquisition of nomenclature, as well as social skills acquisition, through counselling on topics of social and/or sexual behavior given by care providers and the facilitators.

Treatment of Other DSM-III-R Diagnoses

Considerable psychological treatment was rendered through Group Process in concert with the Educator's goals. However, in-home, clinical services were delivered 1:1 with each client who needed it, ranging from one-four sessions/month, and some treatment objectives were coordinated with care providers in the clients' homes. These services were useful to identify some potential subjects who were referred for treatment but found to be without pathology and with the skills to avoid sex offenses. Therefore, they were excluded from unnecessarily expensive services.

Of the eight subjects, only four could also be diagnosed with a disorder, in addition to a mental handicapping condition, that could be accommodated through the treatments described here (see Table 1). One man, with a social phobia, was treated through desensitization to more and more sophisticated social situations until his disorder remitted. There was a strong association between remission of his disorder and his acquisition of culturally normative social behaviors that, we believe, rendered him no longer a danger to the community. Two other subjects fulfilled the criteria for a diagnosis of pedophilia. Treatment of these had two foci. First, they were helped to recognize antecedents to offending behavior. Then, treatment was rendered through shaping a repertoire of self-control strategies that the subjects could use when they perceived antecedents for their pedophillic offending behavior. A fourth subject presented with post-traumatic stress disorder that apparently developed during his incarceration; Group Process was helpful with the cognitive-behavioral treatment strategies being used to reduce the symptoms of his disorder. A product of therapy was that he was able to develop remorse for victims of sexual assault; this may be useful for therapeutic maintenance.

Employment Gains

Other positive outcomes were observed in the area of vocational improvement. Most of the participants experienced some significant improvement in their work situation. For some, it was simply not having to suffer the consequences of inappropriate sexual expression at work. For others, it meant a step into less highly supervised and supported positions. Improved employment experiences have resulted in higher self-esteem, higher wages and more independence for these participants. These gains represent significant improvements over past patterns of behavior and staff who work with them can focus more upon skills acquisition instead of maladaptive behavior suppression.

Living Gains

Another area of improvement for some of the group members was in their residential experience. Two of the men moved out of highly supervised group homes and returned to live with family members. These changes were only agreed to by the facilitators and case management agencies after these individuals demonstrated the acquisition of skills necessary to remain "safe" in the community. A third participant remained in his group home and, with the assistance of the facilitators, his parents and his case manager, he has brokered a new living arrangement whereby privacy was granted him two times per day, if he chose. Unfortunately, masturbation is oftentimes the sole culturally normative sexual expression possible for many adults with developmental disabilities, given the difficulties (logistical and discriminatory) which face this population in developing intimate relationships.

DISCUSSION

Our impression is that men with mental retardation differ significantly from men without a diagnosed disability in their culpability as alleged sex offenders. For example, only two of the men in the sample, of eight who had been alleged to have molested children, fulfilled DSM-III-R clinical criteria for Pedophilia after clinical diagnostic work ups had been completed. All eight men who had been alleged to have histories of child molestation did not reoffend during the 34 months after comprehensive clinical, educational, and group therapy/educational services began.

These sample data, along with the results of others (e.g., Demetral, 1989; Swanson & Garwick, 1990) should be offered as evidence to counter the impressions, without data, of Gebhard (1977) and previous authors who intimated that men with mental retardation were at high risk of committing sex offenses. These data, taken with others, also strongly suggest that the intellectual capability of alleged sex offenders, particularly those charged with Child Molestation, be assessed and then taken into account during the arraignment process. The potential use of this process might be to be able to triage mentally handicapped persons into treatment/educational programs that could render them at considerably lower risk to citizens rather than incarcerate them or, in some other way, leave them without treatment services.

Sexual misbehavior arises from a complex web of personal and societal forces. Given our small sample and the infancy of this type of treatment for men with developmental disabilities, our conclusions must be provisional until longitudinal studies have been published concerning the effectiveness of small group treatment for this population. However, a few conclusions can be made.

First, it is important to enlist qualified facilitators who have considerable experience serving people with developmental disabilities. Essential are a person who is expert in dealing with the clinical issues of this population and a person experienced in instructing people with developmental disabilities in sexuality. A third facilitator representing daily contact with the group members is also highly desirable and probably impacts positively the degree to which gains made in group are generalized to participants' daily lives.

Second, there is a tremendous need for human service delivery systems to provide greater social opportunities for people with developmental disabilities (Hingsburger, 1989). Normative sexual expression will never replace obnoxious behavior until this population has equal access to adult relationship formation (Hingsburger et al., 1991). The skills necessary to build a satisfying social/sexual relationship cannot be taught in a vacuum. For example, teaching and rehearsing the skills necessary for dating becomes simply an exercise in frustration without the advocacy usually necessary to make it possible for two adults with developmental disabilities to actually go on a date. Until people with developmental disabilities are viewed as legitimate adults, granted the same rights, responsibilities and freedoms with regard to controlling their social and sexual lives, the need for treatment of this kind will continue to grow — and continue to be limited in its effectiveness by having only autoerotic sexual expression to offer as an alternative to illegal sexual activity.

Third, the enlistment of residential/family and vocational/day program support is critical in reinforcing the group treatment of the participants. Individual behavioral change cannot be made manifest without a matrix of support. Family members, care providers, social workers and other significantly supportive people must be committed to promoting the participant's growth and maintenance of culturally normative sexual expression. For example, assistance in creating greater opportunities for adult relationship formation and intimate relationship formation is a crucial part of the participant's ability to steer clear of committing grave sexual mistakes. Conversely, when significant others have lacked the motivation to support behavioral changes, participants' prognoses for improved behavior have been significantly diminished.

Fourth, it has been our experience that adults with developmental disabilities have the potential to approximate culturally acceptable modes of sexual expression and will usually endeavor to do so, given both the necessary education and the opportunities. Further, we have found that the participants in our group misbehaved sexually due to a lack of education and opportunity to express their sexuality (Hingsburger et al., 1991).

Finally, we feel that vastly greater success with this population, using a small group treatment format but based in an overall service delivery plan grounded in the needs of the individual, seems likely if others are willing to muster the necessary resources and further refine this model of treatment. Research into larger, long-term projects that serve individuals with development disabilities who sexually misbehave should be conducted and reported. Since they are less mobile and they are already enrolled for services through a case management agency, it may be possible for better long term, follow up studies to be done on men with mental retardation than on nonhandicapped persons.

REFERENCES

Adams, G. L., Tallorn, R. J., & Alcorn, D. A. (1982). Attitudes toward the sexuality of mentally retarded and nonretarded persons. *Education and Training of the Mentally Retarded. 17,* 307-312.

Demetral, D. (1989). Adult developmentally disabled sex offender treatment group program at Valley Mountain Regional Center, Stockton, CA.

Dwyer, S.M., & Meyers, S. (1990). Sex offender treatment: A six month to ten-year follow up study. *Annals of Sex Research, 3,* 305-318.

Dwyer, M., & Rosser, B.R.S. (1992). Treatment outcome research cross-referencing a six-month to ten-year follow-up study on sex offenders. *Annals of Sex Research, 5,* 87-97.

Gebhard, P.H. (1977). Sex offenders. In J. Money & H. Musaph (Eds.), *Handbook of sexology.* (Pp. 1088-1094). Elsevier: North-Holland.

Greer, J.G., & Stuart, J.R. (1983). *The sexual aggressor.* New York: Van Nostrand Reinhold.

Griffiths, D. M., Quinsey, V. L., & Hingsburger, D. (1989) *Changing inappropriate sexual behavior,* Baltimore: Brooks.

Groth, N. (1979). *Men who rape: The psychology of the offender.* New York: Plenum.

Haaven, J., Little, R., & Petre-Miller, D. (1990). *Treating intellectually disabled sex offenders: a model residential program.* Orwell, Vermont: Safer Society Press.

Hall, J.E. (1975). Sexuality and the mentally retarded. In J.R. Green (Ed.), *Human sexuality: A health practitioner's text* (Pp. 165-174). Baltimore: Williams & Wilkins.

Hingsburger, D. (1989). Relationship training, sexual behavior, and persons with developmental handicaps. *Psychiatric Aspects of Mental Retardation Reviews, 8 (5),* 33-37.

Hingsburger, D., Griffiths, D., & Quinsey, V. (1991). Detecting counterfeit sexual deviance from sexual inappropriateness. *Habilitative Mental Health Care Newsletter, 10 (9),* 51-54.

Kempton, W. (1993). *Socialization and sexuality: A comprehensive training guide for professionals helping people with disabilities that hinder learning.* Philadelphia: W. Kempton.

Korinek, L., & Polloway, E. (1993). Social skills: Review and implications for instruction for students with mild mental retardation. *Strategies for teaching students with mild to severe mental retardation.* R. Gable and S. Warren (Eds.). (Pp. 120-131). Baltimore: Brooks.

Leyin, A., & Dicks, M. (1987). Assessment and evaluation: assessing what we are doing. In A. Craft (Ed.) *Mental handicap and sexuality: issues and perspectives.* (Pp. 139-157). New York: Costello.

Losada-Paisey, G., & Paisey, T.J.H. (1988). Program evaluation of a comprehensive treatment package for mentally retarded sex offenders. *Behavioral Residential Treatment, 3(4),* 247-265.

Lund, C. A. (1992) Long term treatment of sexual behavior problems in adolescent and adult developmentally disabled persons, *Annals of Sex Research, 5,* 5-31.

Monat-Haller, R. K. (1992). *Understanding and expressing sexuality.* Baltimore: Brooks.

Muccigrosso, L. (1991). Sexual abuse prevention strategies and programs for persons with developmental disabilities. *Journal of Sexuality and Disability, 9(3),* 261-271.

Muccigrosso, L., Scavarda, M., Simpson-Brown, R., & Thallacker, B. (1991). *Double jeopardy: Pregnant and parenting youth in special education.* Reston, VA: Council for Exceptional Children.

Nolley, D.A. (1975). Problems of sexuality among the mentally retarded at a large state institution. Paper presented at the Council for Exceptional Children, Grand Rapids, MI.

Nolley, D.A. (1978). Treatment of aberrant sexuality in the mentally retarded. Paper presented at the American Association on Mental Deficiency, Denver.

Pfadt, A. (1991). Psychotherapy with mentally retarded adults: Issues related to design, implementation, and evaluation, *Research in Developmental Disabilities, 12,* 261-285.

Prendergast, W.E. (1991). *Treating Sex Offenders in Correctional Institutions and Outpatient Clinics: A Guide to Clinical Practice.* New York: The Haworth Press, Inc.

Senn, C. (1988) Sex offenders with intellectual impairments. In C. Senn (Ed.) *Vulnerable,* (Pp. 53-61). Toronto: Roeher Institute.

Stanfield, J. (1990). *Life Facts I: Sexuality.* Santa Barbara, CA: James Stanfield.

Swanson, C.K., & Garwick, G.B. (1990). Treatment for low-functioning sex offenders: Group therapy and interagency coordination. *Mental Retardation, 28(3),* 155-161.

Weinrott, M.R., & Saylor, M. (1991). Self report of crimes committed by sex offenders. *Journal of Interpersonal Violence, 6,* 286-300.

Woodvale Management Services (1989). *The Woodvale Sexuality Assessment and Curriculum Guide.* Austin, MN: Author.

AUTHORS' NOTES

David Nolley, PhD, is a licensed psychologist and partner with Lyne Muccigrosso, a sex educator, in Family Life Associates of Northern California, with offices in San Jose and Los Gatos. Eric Zigman is program manager with the Skills Center, Santa Cruz.

The authors gratefully acknowledge the assistance of Andy Pereira of the Skills Center and Dr. Dan Downey, San Andreas Regional Center, San Jose.

Address correspondence to Dr. David Nolley, 20432 Silverado, Suite 214, Cupertino, CA 95014.

Why Therapy Fails with Some Sex Offenders: Learning Difficulties Examined Empirically

RON LANGEVIN
Juniper Psychological Services, Etobicoke, Ontario

DENNIS MARENTETTE
Juniper Psychological Services, Etobicoke, Ontario

BRUNO ROSATI
Juniper Psychological Services, Etobicoke, Ontario

ABSTRACT A total of 203 men accused of sexual offenses were compared on the Wechsler Adult Intelligence Scale (WAIS-R), the Halstead-Reitan Battery, school grade repeats and therapy outcome measures that included desire for treatment, attendance, and attitude to treatment. There were 75 intrafamilial and 54 extrafamilial child sexual abusers, 41 sexual aggressives and 43 miscellaneous sex offenders. Results showed that 52% were school dropouts and 53% had failed at least one grade in school. Although the group's intelligence was in the average range, 33% scored in the impaired range of the Halstead-Reitan Battery. Of the therapy outcome measures, only attitude to therapy was related to the Reitan Impairment Index, with more impaired individuals evincing a more negative attitude to therapy. Sex offenders with and without learning problems did not differ in desire for treatment, but those with learning problems had better attendance. Approaches to improving therapy success with clients who have learning difficulties are discussed. *[Copies of this paper are available from The Haworth Document Delivery Service: 1-800-342-9678.]*

When Hucker, Langevin, and Bain (1988) attempted to evaluate the effectiveness of Provera as a treatment for sex offenders in a double blind study, they found that treatment compliance was a major factor to be addressed in treatment success. They offered Provera or a placebo to 100 consecutive pedophilic offenders. Only 48 acknowledged that they had a problem and wished to entertain *any* treatment plans. Eighteen agreed to take Provera for 3 months but only 11 successfully finished the trial program. Thus, an evaluation of Provera itself was seriously hampered by the noncompliance of the offenders studied. One can see that not only were sex offenders unwilling to take Provera, over half could not acknowledge a need for therapeutic intervention.

In a further effort to evaluate why this was so, Langevin, Wright, and Handy (1988) asked 87 sex offenders if they wanted treatment and what type they would like. Only 49% wanted treatment. The most preferred therapy was individual psychotherapy (89%). The most frequently used therapy for sex offenders, namely aversive conditioning, was the least acceptable (less than 10% acceptance), along with castration (1%), and sex drive-reducing drug therapy (less than 16%, with Provera included). Group therapy had a mixed rating; it was both very desired by some (24%) and seen as undesirable by others (7%). Less than 2-in-5 of the sex offenders considered their sexual behavior to be a problem.

The results of this study suggested that there was considerable disparity between therapists' *application* of treatment and the offenders' *perception* of their own needs. The authors recommended that improving *congruence* between therapist and patient goals may enhance treatment compliance and success for sex offenders in general. The present study is an attempt to examine another factor that may play a significant role in desire for treatment and in treatment compliance, namely the capabilities of the client to learn.

Over the last three years, we have treated federal parolees who have a variety of problems; among them is a history of learning problems which we were concerned might interfere with learning in therapy. In an earlier examination of 76 sex offenders (25 incest perpetrators, 25 pedophilic offenders, and 26 sexual aggressives), half or more of each group had failed a grade in school (56% incest, 48% pedophilic, and 86%

of sexual aggressives failed at least 1 school grade) suggesting early learning difficulties (cf. Langevin & Pope, 1993).

Learning difficulties are important to therapy in at least two ways. First, the individual may not be capable of processing the information in therapy that is suitable for a person of average intelligence. Second, an individual who has learning difficulties may develop an attitude towards learning situations and, in particular, avoid classroom type experiences where they may have met failure and derision from other students. Learning difficulties (LD) can also be associated with poor self-esteem that may lead to avoidance of therapy as well. Many clients with learning difficulties have been subjected to a lifetime of abuse because of their problems. In effect, the individual with learning problems may tell himself "I may be stupid but I'm not crazy, I don't need a psychiatrist or psychologist." It is natural to avoid aversive situations and the learning environment may be one such situation. It is possible that such attitudes play a role in therapy acceptance and compliance.

The presence of learning difficulties has long been recognized as a factor that is more prevalent in the criminal population and might even be considered criminogenic (cf. Buikhuisen, van der Plas-Korenhoff & Bontekoe, 1985). Robins, West, and Herjanic (1975), for example, examined 67 males, their school and police records, and those of their sons as well. They found a relationship between index cases, deviant behavior, failure of the sons to complete high school, and tendency of the sons to engage in delinquency.

It is doubtful that a simple relationship exists between level of intellectual functioning or learning difficulties and committing criminal offenses. But some studies have suggested there is an over-representation of learning problems among criminals, and this surmise was investigated as a possible factor that might influence treatment compliance.

The purposes of the present study were twofold. *First,* the cognitive abilities and learning problems among sex offenders were documented to evaluate the exact numbers of such cases and the extent to which this may be an issue for therapists treating sex offenders. *Second,* individuals with learning difficulties were evaluated in terms of their desire for treatment and treatment compliance.

• **Table 1: Subjects Arrayed by Offense**

	N	%
Incest Offenders	75	37
Pedophilia Offenders	54	27
Sexual Aggressives	41	20
Miscellaneous	33	17
Total	203	

METHOD

Subjects

The most recent 203 files from Juniper Psychological Services were examined (Table 1). All files were selected regardless of the offense category represented. Subjects fell into two basic categories: (1) legal referrals, either from lawyers or crown attorneys (accounting for 60% of the total of 203), and (2) federal parolees (40%), who were seen as part of a treatment program for sex offenders in our clinic. All cases were male. The sample consisted of 75 intrafamilial child sexual abusers (incest perpetrators); 54 extrafamilial child sexual abusers (pedophilic offenders); 41 sexual aggressives (offenders against adult females); and 43 miscellaneous offenders (mostly courtship disorders, such as exhibitionists).

The average age of the sample was 38.38 years (SD = 12.10); the youngest case was 14 and the oldest 84. There was a trend to significant group differences in age, with incest offenders (Mean = 38.50) and pedophiles (Mean = 39.55) being somewhat older than sexual aggressives (Mean = 34.07) and miscellaneous cases (Mean = 36.42), as expected (F = 2.21, df = 4, 193, p = .0699).

Procedure

The files were searched for information that is routinely collected as part of the assessment. In particular, the Verbal, Performance, and Full IQ scores from the Wechsler Adult Intelligence Scale (WAIS-R) and the Halstead-Reitan Battery Impairment Index (0 = Not impaired, or score of 0.50 or less; 1 = Impaired, or score of 0.51 or more) were tabulated.

• *Figure 1: Educational Level of Offenders Studied*

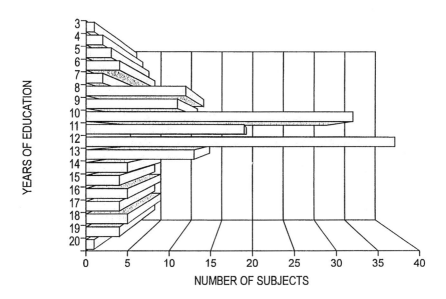

In addition, it was determined from other clinical materials which individuals had learning problems in school or had failed a grade in school
(0 = No, 1 = Yes). In 126 cases a treatment questionnaire had been
administered asking, among other things, whether the individuals wanted
treatment or not (0 = No, 1 = Yes). Details are presented in Langevin et
al., 1988.

   Simkin, Ward, Bowman, and Rinck (1989) examined treatment outcome in 122 clients prior to their entry into therapy and found that denial
as measured by the Multiphasic Sex Inventory (MSI) was a good predictor of treatment compliance. They also examined an overall therapy score
that included attendance, number of therapy goals attained, therapist
rating of attitude and behavior of the client, and likelihood of recidivism.

- *Figure 2: Proportion of Offenders Who Failed in School by Grade Failed*

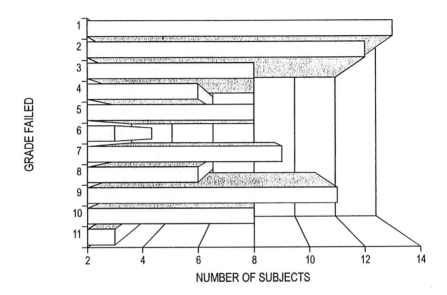

In their data, attendance at therapy appeared to be most important of these variables.

In the present study, two factors were examined, therapy attendance and attitude to therapy, which overlaps with Simkins et al., attitudes and behavior ratings of therapists.

Two therapists rated their cases for (1) attendance (dichotomously scored at 0 = poor attendance, 1 = good attendance), and (2) attitude to treatment. The latter score indicated whether the client had a negative attitude to therapy, expressing a desire not to be in treatment and showed a failure to work on significant treatment issues. Some men were initially resistant but changed during treatment while others were negative or positive from the outset. Thus, three subgroups were identified for attitude to therapy: negative, positive, and changed attitudes to treatment.

• Table 2: Learning Disabled Subjects Arrayed by Offense

	N	% Learning Disabled
Incest Offenders	66	56
Pedophilia Offenders	43	42
Sexual Aggressives	27	67
Miscellaneous	11	55

The results were analyzed using Chi Square tests as well as Oneway Analyses of Variance to compare variables of interests. Number of cases may vary depending on the availability of the information. Not all information is collected on all cases, but is a function of the type of referral.

RESULTS

Of the 162 cases where the information was available, the average number of grade years completed at school was 11.43 (SD = 3.16). As seen in Figure 1. Forty-eight (30%) had completed grade 12 or grade 13 (36 and 12 cases respectively). Many of the men (52%) dropped out of high school. An additional 29 individuals (18%) had po st-secondary education. Ten individuals (6%) had grade 7 or less education. Thus, the sample is a mixed one in terms of education.

In the Ontario Educational System, it is unusual that a child would be retained in a grade. Policy dictates that "it is better to have child with his age peers." In spite of this, 50% of our sample had repeated a grade. Sixty-one (43%) men had failed one grade, 20 (14%) had failed two grades, and 5 (3.5%) had failed three or more grades (Total n = 141). Seven additional men were in Special Education as children, indicating that they were identified as having learning problems by the schools, even though there were no grade failures. Overall, 53% had learning problems as children that led to failed grades or placement in a special class.

As Figure 2 shows, the grades failed were, for the most part, in grade school or the early years of education. Only one individual failed grade 11, 4 individuals failed grade 10, the bulk of failures (76%) occurred between grades 1 and 8, indicating that these individuals were retained

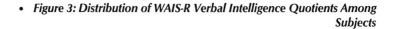

• *Figure 3: Distribution of WAIS-R Verbal Intelligence Quotients Among Subjects*

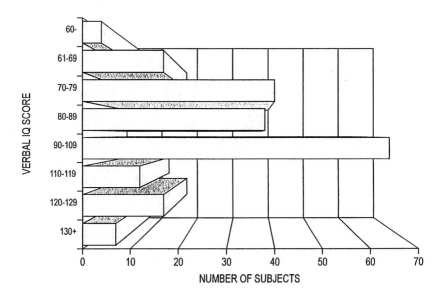

in school at an early stage of their educational careers for one reason or another.

In some cases there were emotional factors, i.e., family disturbance, mental illness, or hyperactivity which may have played a role in the decision to fail the child but many cases showed learning difficulties that appear to have a cognitive basis, as seen in the subsequent data.

There were no statistically significant sex offender subgroup differences in learning difficulties (LD), although sexual aggressives had the most LD cases (67%), as shown in Table 2.

It appears that individuals who had served time in federal penitentiary and committed more serious crimes were more likely to have LD (61%) than those who were referred legally (44%) and were seen pre-sentence (A data trend is noted; Chi Square = 3.53, df = 1, p < .0608.)

- **Table 3: Coefficients of Correlation between Learning Disability, Cognitive Impairment, and Intelligence among Sex Offenders**

	1	2	3	4	5	6
1 = Grade Failure						
2 = Verbal Intelligence	-.36					
3 = Performance Intelligence	-.21	.67				
4 = Reitan Impairment	.29	-.44	-.53			
5. = Desire for Treatment	.08	.07	.10	-.03		
6 = Treatment Attendance	.33	.18	-.18	-.04	.00	
7 = Attitude toward Treatm ent	.32	.10	.10	-.28	.37	.33

The average full IQ on the WAIS-R was 97.96 (SD = 16.54) indicating that the sample overall was of average intelligence. However, compared to Wechsler's distribution of scores for the WAIS-R, the present results for Verbal IQ were significantly different (Figure 3). In particular, there were more cases than expected in the borderline range of intelligence (i.e., IQ = 70-79), fewer in the bright-normal (110-119), and surprisingly more in the 130-140 range. Although this may reflect the peculiarities of the clientele seen, other results (Mohr, Turner, and Jerry, 1964) have also suggested that the IQ of some sex offenders, i.e., pedophiles, may skew to the lower end of normal. In spite of the referral sources, some individuals are going to have learning difficulties that may be a factor in their comprehension during the therapy process.

Halstead-Reitan Neuropsychological testing was available on 159 persons. Of these, 53 (33%) scored in the impaired range, further indicating that neurocognitive deficits in one third of the sex offenders are important considerations.

Table 3 shows that grade failure was negatively related to education and intelligence (slightly more so to verbal intelligence) but positively related to neuropsychological impairment. Thus cognitive deficits can be considered a partial explanation for grade failure and LD but not the whole answer.

Desire for Treatment

One hundred and twenty-six men had answered a treatment questionnaire. Of concern here was the issue of whether the client felt he needed treatment at the time of assessment. Only 30% said that they did. This result was not significantly influenced by group membership, i.e., whether they were incest offenders or sexual aggressives, etc. It was unrelated to repeating a grade in school, to their intelligence level, or academic achievement.

That only 30% of the men wanted to be in treatment is somewhat lower than previous results reported (e.g., Langevin et al., 1988) in which 49% desired treatment. More federal parolees wanted treatment (39%) compared to legal referrals (25%). Overall results, however, continue to indicate that motivation for treatment is a major problem facing treatment providers of sex offenders.

Attendance

Data were available only on 34 cases. Attendance was good for 14 (41%). Those with learning difficulties (LD) were better attenders (n = 24, 50% good attendance) and those without learning problems (non-LD) were poorer attenders (n = 10, 20% good attendance).

Attendance was not significantly related to education, intelligence, Reitan Impairment Index, or desire for treatment, but was positively correlated with age. It was correlated with attitude to treatment, indicating that those with good attendance had a positive attitude toward treatment. However, there was only a 14% relationship between Desire for treatment and Attitude to therapy and an 11% relationship between Treatment Attendance and Attitude to Treatment, indicating that therapy indices were, for the most part, unique.

Attitude Toward Treatment

Overall, 15% (n = 5) had a positive attitude toward treatment initially and 50% (n = 17) were initially negative but changed over the course of treatment. Thirty-five percent (n = 12) had negative attitudes which they maintained till the end. There was a significant difference between LD and non-LD groups. Again Ns are small but more LD cases changed (58%) or had positive attitudes throughout (21%) compared to non-LD cases who were more often negative throughout (70%) or changed (30%) (Chi Square = 8.05, df = 2, p < .02).

Attitude toward therapy was not significantly related to education or intelligence but was negatively correlated with the Reitan Impairment Index. That is, those men who showed significant neuropsychological impairment had more negative attitudes to therapy. As shown in Table 3, the Reitan Impairment Index was positively related to grade failure but the overlap of the two variables was small (9%).

DISCUSSION

The results of the present study indicate that substantial numbers of the sex offenders studied had learning problems. Over one half have repeated early grades in school or were placed in Special Education classes, and one third suffered from serious neurocognitive impairment. One may wish to speculate about the etiological significance of these findings, given some research suggesting the presence of brain damage and dysfunction in sex offenders (cf. Langevin, Wortzman, Wright, and Handy, 1989). However, it is possible that sex offenders are no different from criminals in general who may also show more cognitive deficits than the population at large. One may also postulate that one sees a biased sample in offenders who are caught (i.e., the brighter ones get away; cf. Langevin and Lang, 1990, for a discussion of this topic and related issues).

We have not taken into account the influence of other cultures on the results. Canada is clearly a multi-cultural society at present and future analysis will examine this factor as well as the role of parenting in school performance. Biological factors may also contribute to therapy attitude, e.g., the presence of diabetes (cf. Langevin & Bain, 1992).

Regardless of the cognitive abilities of a random sample of sex offenders, the ones who are caught (and they are the ones usually seen by therapists) often have cognitive deficits and learning difficulties which may interfere with the therapy process. In a small sample (n = 34) of therapy cases, 24 (71%) had learning difficulties and 79% had negative attitudes to therapy initially but 58% changed to a positive attitude. It is interesting that the most seriously *cognitively impaired* (Reitan Impairment Index) had negative attitudes to therapy.

Attempts have been made to overcome LD offenders' attitudes to therapy and improve their cooperation by

❑ Dealing with the LD upfront and asking about their attitude to treatment.

❑ Dealing with *their* issues first, rather than the therapist's (which translates into dealing with employment and living arrangements/family before sex problems).

❑ Using a "client-centered" problem solving approach in which their solutions and abilities are emphasized over the "canned relapse prevention or assertiveness program."

❑ Rewarding their strengths rather than focusing on their weaknesses (cf. Langevin et al., 1988; Langevin & Pope, 1993).

The present results indicate the importance of reaching the LD client because it is possible they commit more serious crimes. More LD cases came from federal prisons and it would be valuable to study whether their crimes are more violent, if they recidivate more, or have more adjustment difficulties both in prison and upon return to the community. The role of LD in crime may suggest prevention strategies as well as earlier intervention for a select group of youths.

The present results in a small sample of therapy cases suggest that interventions can be effective in changing compliance and attitudes to therapy in learning disabled sex offenders.

REFERENCES

Buikhuisen, W., van der Plas-Korenhoff, C., & Bontekoe, E.H. (1985). Parental home and deviance. *International Journal of Offender Therapy & Comparative Criminology, 29,* 201-210.

Fishman, L.T. (1986). Repeating the cycle of hard living and crime: Wives' accommodations to husbands' parole performance. *Federal Probation, 50,* 44-54.

Hucker, S., Langevin, R., & Bain, J. (1988). A double blind trial of Provera for pedophiles. *Annals of Sex Research, 1,* 227-242.

Kolvin, I., Miller, F.J.W., Fleeting, M., & Kolvin, P.A. (1988). Social and parenting factors affecting criminal offence rates. *British Journal of Psychiatry, 152,* 80-90.

Langevin, R., & Bain, J. (1992). Diabetes in sex offenders. *Annals of Sex Research, 5,* 99-118.

Langevin, R., & Lang, R.A. (1990) . Substance abuse among sex offenders. *Annals of Sex Research, 3,* 397-424.

Langevin R., & Pope, S. (1993). Working with learning disabled sex offenders. *Annals of Sex Research, 6* (in press).

Langevin, R., Wortzman, G., Wright, P., & Handy, L. (1989). Studies of brain damage and dysfunction in sex offenders. *Annals of Sex Research, 2,* 163-179.

Langevin, R., Wright, P., & Handy, L. (1988). What treatment do sex offenders want? *Annals of Sex Research, 1,* 363-386.

Mohr, J., Turner, R.E., & Jerry, M. (1964). *Pedophilia and exhibitionism.* Toronto: University of Toronto Press.

Robins, L.N., West, P.A., & Herjanic, B.L., (1975). Arrests and delinquency in two generations: A study of black urban families and their children. *Journal of Child Psychology and Psychiatry, 16,* 125-140.

Simkins, L., Ward, W., Bowman, S., & Rinck, C.M. (1989). The Multiphasic Sex Inventory: Diagnosis and prediction of treatment response in child sexual abusers. *Annals of Sex Research, 2,* 205-226.

AUTHORS' NOTES

Ron Langevin, Ph.D., is director of Juniper Psychological Services in Etobicoke, Ontario, and associate professor, Department of Psychiatry, University of Toronto. He has researched sexual offenders for 24 years and has authored *Sexual Strands: Understanding and Treating Sexual Anomalies in Men* and more-recently edited *Sex Offenders & Their Victims.*

Dennis Marentette is on staff at Juniper Psychological Services. He holds a Master of Divinity degree from the University of Toronto and is presently enrolled at York University.

Bruno Rosati is a University of Toronto graduate pursuing a degree in psychology and currently is on staff at Juniper Psychological Services.

Address correspondence to Dr. Ron Langevin, Suite 200, Dundas Kipling Center, 5353 Dundas Street W., Etobicoke, Ontario, Canada.

SEX OFFENDER TREATMENT
Biological Dysfunction, Intrapsychic Conflict, Interpersonal Violence. Pp. 157-177.

Sex Offenders in Treatment: Variations in Remodeling and Their Therapeutic Implications

ROCHELLE A. SCHEELA
Bemidji State University

ABSTRACT This research is an extension of a grounded theory study conducted to explore incest offender perceptions of treatment in order to generate an explanatory theory of the sexual abuse treatment process. In the original study, methodology included 20 audio-taped interviews, direct observations of 65 therapy groups, and record analysis. The subjects were a theoretical sampling of 20 adult male incest offenders currently in, graduates of, and drop-outs of, a community sexual abuse treatment program. Constant comparative analysis (Glaser and Strauss, 1967; Strauss and Corbin, 1990) was used to collect and analyze the data concurrently. A remodeling process was identified by the men involving the offenders' worlds falling apart, the offenders taking on the project of remodeling themselves, tearing out the damaged parts, rebuilding themselves, their relationships, and their environments, doing the upkeep to maintain the remodeling that has been accomplished and, moving on to new remodeling projects as they progress through treatment. Further analysis of these data as well as an additional 22 interviews, observations, and record analysis of other types of sex offenders indicate that offenders experience the remodeling process in a variety of ways with implications for treatment strategies and outcomes. *[Copies of this paper are available from The Haworth Document Delivery Service: 1-800-342-9678.]*

Researchers typologize sex offenders in different ways based on etiology, motivation, and/or types of abuse(s). However, none address a typology of offenders in the treatment process. The purpose of this study is to identify various types of sex offenders based on how they vary in the remodeling treatment process and the treatment implications of these variations.

REVIEW OF THE LITERATURE

The sex offender literature posits several different sex offender typologies. Groth, Hobson, and Gary (1982), based on 16 years of professional experience with over 500 offenders, classify child molesters into a fixated or regressed typology. A regressed offender turns to a child as an adult substitute when adults are not available or do not meet his needs, whereas the fixated offender turns to a child as a way of remaining a child himself.

Knight and Prentky (1990) describe nine types of rapists based on their motivation and level of social competence. Types one and two involve opportunistic rapists with high and low levels of social competence. Type three is a pervasively angry offender. Types four, five, six and seven are sexually motivated rapists, but differ in terms of the sadistic quality of the offense and the level of social competence. Types eight and nine are vindictively motivated and involve low to moderate social competence.

Larson and Maddock (1986) describe a typology of four family abusive styles based on the underlying purpose of the abuse. In the *affection-exchange* family type, sexual abuse stems from the the need for affection on the part of the offender and often the victim as well. The *erotic-exchange* family sexualizes everything, and thus sex within the family may be seen as a right. The *aggression-exchange* type of family sexual abuse is often an extension of physical abuse; the sexual abuse being a form of punishment and humiliation. The *rage-expression* family abusive style is highly violent and the most akin to sadistic rape.

A significant number of researchers are concluding that there is no one type of sexual offender (Blanchard, 1989; Bolton, Morris, and Mac-Eachron, 1989; Conte, 1990; Salter, 1988). Conte (1990) identifies problems with the fixated and regressed typology. First, it was developed with an incarcerated sample of offenders, and these men may be very different from other types of offenders. Also, he states there is no evidence to support this typology; community therapists report that the offenders they work with have characteristics of both, and thus, represent a mixed group.

Langevin, Handy, Russon, and Day (1985) compared 34 incestuous fathers, 32 heterosexual pedophiles with no history of incest, and 54 men with no history of any offenses who served as a control group, and found that it would be hard to specify characteristics of incest offenders as they represent a very heterogeneous group. The stereotypes of dirty old man, stranger, retarded, chemically dependent, sexually frustrated, and increasingly violent over time are incorrect. Offenders vary considerably in characteristics, abuse and criminal/mental health history, and social skills. They are a complex, heterogeneous group with no classic characteristics (Ballard, Blair, Devereaux, Valentine, Horton, and Johnson, 1990; Bolton et al., 1989; Herman, 1981; Horton, Johnson, Roundy, and Williams, 1990; Langevin, Handy, Russon, and Day, 1985).

Abel, Becker, Cunningham-Rathner, Mittelman, and Rouleau (1988) conducted a descriptive study using the self-reports of 561 non-incarcerated sex offenders voluntarily seeking evaluation and/or treatment at the University of Tennessee Center for the Health Sciences and the New York State Psychiatric Institute. They found that most offenders had significant experience with as many as ten different types of deviant sexual behavior without regard, in many cases, to gender, age, and familial relationship of the victim. Confidentiality was guaranteed, a structured clinical interview was done, specific questions were asked, and a full history was obtained. This is perhaps why the rates of deviant behavior were so high.

Conte (1985) suggests that instead of trying to fit sex offenders into specific types, it is more useful to think of them in terms of a number of clinical dimensions such as denial, sexual arousal, sexual fantasies, cognitive distortions, social skill deficits, and other problems.

THEORETICAL FRAMEWORK

The above mentioned typologies focus primarily on motivation, etiology, and/or types of abuse(s). The intent of this study is to look at a treatment process typology using the remodeling process, a theoretical framework generated from a grounded theory study of adult male incest offenders in an outpatient treatment program (Scheela, 1992-a, -b). The informants described the process they experience as they progress through treatment as a remodeling.

Metaphorically, the offenders see themselves as carpenters and their remodeling, or rehabilitation, as customized work. Some offenders remodel one space at a time, completely finishing one room before moving onto another. Others remodel several rooms at the same time. Some remodel only certain rooms, others gut the whole inside of their psychological structure and rebuild. Some patch the leaks or cover the cracks or slap a quick coat of paint over the damaged parts, and don't really remodel at all. Some build walls or fences around their houses and don't want any part of remodeling. Remodeling as metaphor is a safe way for the offenders to regard the healing process; the old foundation and some of the framework will always be there (history, memories, personality disorders, intelligence, the abuse). The foundation may be strengthened and fortified, but not totally removed or re-done. The offender is not cured, and thus must always guard against reoffending.

Remodeling, as the offenders described and named it, involves the dynamic, overlapping, nonlinear processes of *falling apart, taking on, tearing out, rebuilding, doing the upkeep, and moving on.* The offenders described their worlds *falling apart* emotionally and physically once the abuse was disclosed and they were forced to face the consequences. They described intense physical reactions such as anorexia, insomnia, nausea and vomiting, weight loss, uncontrollable crying, and chest pain. The symptoms were life-threatening for some offenders. The offenders also talked about falling apart emotionally. They experienced shock and disbelief at what had happened and confusion regarding what would happen to them and their families. The offenders expressed fear of incarceration, the unknown, and of losing everything, but felt helplessness to do anything to help themselves. They felt intense guilt and shame because of the public humiliation they experienced and because of the "horrible deed" they had done.

Paradoxically, offenders talked about experiencing relief, because the abuse was finally out in the open and they would receive help for their problems (Scheela and Stern, in press).

The *taking on* process involved the offenders admitting to the abuse, taking responsibility for it, for working in treatment, and for doing the remodeling. Offenders that never reached the decision to take on the remodeling project or did so only minimally, did not remodel themselves or successfully complete treatment.

As the offenders took on responsibility for the abuse and the remodeling project, they became involved in the *tearing out* process. Tearing out involved the processes of going into themselves to assess the damage, digging through the mess, searching for connections and patterns, sorting out what should stay and what should be removed, and cleaning out the rotten parts.

Rebuilding involved offenders making changes to put their lives back together. They began making changes in themselves, their relationships, and their environment. Although many offenders reported improved relationships with their families, not all the changes in relationships were perceived as positive.

Some offenders felt less close to their families. Sometimes, old relationships didn't survive and new relationships were needed. Some offenders had never experienced a real relationship, and rebuilding involved actively establishing relationships for the first time.

The offenders maintained changes by *doing the upkeep*. They began to see remodeling as a life-long process. They are never cured, so they made plans to identify and get their needs met in healthy ways, and protect themselves from further offending. They also needed to protect themselves from the "perception of guilt." Others in society did not readily forgive the offenders or forget the abuse, and the men had to be careful never to place themselves in situations that might appear suspicious. *Moving on* involved offenders moving on to new issues, tasks, and concerns that needed remodeling, and eventually moving on to a life beyond treatment.

The purpose of this study, using the remodeling framework, is to identify remodeling variations and treatment implications. The research question to which a response was sought was: *What are the remodeling variations of adult male sex offenders in treatment?*

SETTING AND TREATMENT PROGRAM

The mental health center is a comprehensive regional mental health center that has served six counties in upper midwest since 1953. The Sexual Abuse Treatment Program (SAT), begun in 1983, is one of the programs at the center and is operated by a multidisciplinary team. Individuals and/or families participate in SAT either on a voluntary basis or, most frequently, as mandated by the courts. The courts often order an entire family to participate in SAT if the family eventually wants to reunite. The SAT program takes approximately two to two-and-a-half years to complete, and involves the following treatment components:

❑ Individual therapy, as needed.

❑ Group therapy for the offenders (adult male, female, and juvenile), women, adolescents (older and younger, victims as well as the nonoffended), and elementary children (older and younger, victims as well as the nonoffended).

❑ Family therapy, usually involving the mother and children at first, and only later, when the victim and family are ready, does the offender participate.

❑ Couples therapy.

❑ Mothers and daughters group therapy.

❑ Support group for offenders to deal with problems of everyday life as offenders.

❑ Educational group, with weekly educational lectures and training on various topics related to sexual abuse, family dynamics, communication, etc., for adult offenders and another for adolescent offenders.

❑ Aftercare, including individual sessions, outcomes testing, and support group that occur for approximately six months after the offender has officially graduated from the treatment program.

The SAT program assumes the offenders are treatable and worthy of treatment. They have committed serious crimes with long-lasting effects on themselves, their victims and families, and possibly many others, and they must take full responsibility for those crimes and damages. No other person or thing is responsible for the abuse. However, the offenders are human beings worthy of treatment; they are more than just their abusive actions. The offenders are also seen in many ways as victims themselves, and although that does not excuse their abuse of others, it is a factor that must be addressed for them to succeed in treatment and prevent future abuse. Treatment is therapeutic not punitive, and the offenders do not have to enter treatment voluntarily to benefit from the process. However, at some point, offenders must take on the remodeling process to progress in treatment. They must recognize and admit that they have a problem, accept responsibility for their actions, look at their attitudes and values toward sexuality and aggression, and realize that sexual abuse is a repetitive, compulsive behavior over which they must gain control. This problem cannot be cured, but it can be treated; the temptation may not be eliminated, but it can be controlled.

We generally do not accept the following types of offenders into our treatment program. (a) those who have an exclusive sexual orientation to children and no age appropriate partners (the true pedophiles), (b) those who are predatory and calculated towards finding their victims, rather than those who are uncalculated and their victims were just "available" and vulnerable, and (c) those considered untreatable due to lack of any conscience or such deep denial that it is unlikely ever to be broken. Ideally, the offenders deemed untreatable by our outpatient program are referred to in-depth, long-term inpatient treatment in a state hospital or a correctional facility. However, the reality is that some of these "untreatables" receive no treatment if we do not accept them into our program. The reason for this is that there are few inpatient treatment programs available in Minnesota, and the ones that do exist are full and have long waiting lists. There is as much as a year's wait or more for some of the programs. Consequently, we have been accepting more of the "untreatables" and giving them a three month chance to prove they can succeed in a program like ours. We have met with both successes and failures thus far with this approach. More inpatient programs or alternative treatment programs are needed for these types of offenders.

To accomplish the treatment goals, the SAT team has developed treatment tools (or tasks) for the offenders. The first is to tell the whole story of the abuse to the other offenders in the group. This is usually done at one of the first meetings the offender attends, but must be done many other times throughout treatment to thoroughly cover all the details. This task helps the offenders face what they have done and accept responsibility.

An empathy document is a second task required. The offenders must write about specific episodes of abuse as if they were the victims. They must address the thoughts and feelings of the victims before, during, and after the offenses, and also what some of the effects will be for the victims throughout life. The offenders then read these documents in the group and receive feedback. The empathy documents often must be redone several times before they are acceptable to the group and staff. This task forces the offenders to examine what they have really done and develop empathy for the victims. When done well, this task is effective in reducing and/or eliminating denial and rationalizations. It is sometimes the first time they see their actions as abuse and not "loving," as submission rather than consent.

Another task is to write an apology letter to the victims and the families. These letters are shared with the group for feedback and frequently must be revised many times before they are deemed acceptable. Whether or not the letters are sent (or shared face-to-face) is dependent upon the victims' and families' needs and wishes. The apology is another way for the offenders to get in touch with the reality of the crime and become accountable. The goal of writing the letter is to facilitate offenders' acknowledgements of remorse, and it can extend to all the forms of abuse committed, not necessarily just sexual abuse.

Development of communication skills is an important task for the offenders. They need to learn to listen, to identify and express feelings and needs, and to empathize with others. This is an on-going task throughout the treatment program, and the Thursday night educational group focuses on education and training in this area, such as assertiveness training and development of listening skills. Most of the offenders find it extremely difficult to identify their own feelings, much less express them. Some of the training is videotaped so the offenders can observe and evaluate themselves. Application of these skills in real life settings is always emphasized and encouraged. Many assignments are given to increase the chances of this happening. Identification of the abuse cycle is another extremely important task for the offenders. They must identify their impaired thinking and distorted belief systems, their preoccupations and fantasies, their ritualizations, their behaviors, and feelings of unmanageability and despair. Three models are used to assist the offenders in this process, the Sexual Addiction Model (Carnes, 1983), the Sexual Assault Cycle (Ryan and Lane, 1991), and the Vulnerability to Incest

Model (Trepper and Barrett, 1989). Three models are presented because they deal with abuse in different ways, and hence give the offenders some flexibility to choose what fits best for them. The Sexual Addiction Model presents a model similar to the addiction model for alcoholics. The Sexual Assault Cycle deals with the abuse in terms of factors that lead to abuse, factors that may or may not be truly addictive in nature. The Vulnerability to Incest Model is a model for all the factors that must be present for abuse to occur and includes social, environmental, and family as well as individual factors. The offenders are also given the book *Out of the Shadows* (Carnes, 1983) to read. This book delves into sexual addiction and explains the addiction cycle in detail. For those offenders who cannot read, an audiotape of the book is available. Identification of the abuse pattern enables the offenders to really begin to understand sexual abuse and how it occurs, and thus provides a way to understand how to prevent it in the future.

An extensive autobiography is another required task for the offenders. Each man must write a detailed account of his family of origin; his childhood; education; occupational, military, marital, health and medical, and criminal history; and his social and sexual development. These autobiographies are often 80 pages or more, and are read to the group a bit at a time for reactions and feedback. The task encourages the offenders to explore and examine the past in relationship to the present, and recognize life patterns of coping (and not coping) that were factors in the abuse and how to prevent them in the future.

A safe plan is finalized late in the treatment program, although it is worked on throughout treatment. The offenders must put together everything they have learned from all of the other tasks and the group experiences, and come up with plans to prevent future abuse. The safe plan is a detailed document that includes all of the thoughts, feelings, and behaviors that led to the abuse, and strategies to protect and prevent them in the future. It focuses on the offenders accepting the fact that there is no cure for their problems, but that they can take control of their thoughts and behavior. They can make decisions that will reduce their temptations and increase their strength to resist. They can develop appropriate coping skills to deal with life's stresses, and not just switch to other inappropriate behaviors such as gambling, drinking, workaholism, etc. Family members also create their own safe plans, so they are able to identify signs that indicate the offenders may be getting into out of control situations and ways they can protect themselves.

The treatment tools are strategies to assist the offenders in the accomplishment of the treatment goals, and may be completed in a variety of sequences depending on the individual needs of the offenders. If offenders need a more basic and structured approach to accomplish the treatment tasks, the *Pathways Workbook* (Kahn, 1990) is used. *Pathways* is a structured approach for dealing with adolescent sex offenders, but has been found to be very helpful for some of the adult offenders as well, especially the lower functioning ones.

METHOD

Design

The design of this study was grounded theory, a qualitative research method developed by sociologists Glaser and Strauss (1967) that "uses a systematic set of procedures to develop an inductively derived grounded theory about a phenomenon" (Strauss and Corbin, 1990, p. 24). The theory is grounded in reality as antecedent conditions, contexts, intervening conditions, action/interaction strategies, and consequences are identified and analyzed for all data (Strauss and Corbin, 1990).

Subjects

The subjects (called informants in a grounded theory study) for this study were 42 adult male sex offenders (incest offenders, rapists, extrafamilial abusers, exhibitionists, and obscene phone callers) involved voluntarily or by court mandate in the Sexual Abuse Treatment Program (SAT), where the researcher works part-time as a therapist. Demographically, the men presented no distinct profile: 20 to 70 years of age, 6 to 17 years of education, annual incomes from less than $10,000 to $50,000, unemployed and unskilled laborers to professionals, no criminal histories to misdemeanors and felonies, predominantly Caucasians with several Native Americans. These data support researchers' reports of the absence of a distinct sex offender profile (Ballard, Blair, Devereaux, Valentine, Horton, and Johnson, 1990; Bolton et al., 1989; Conte, 1985, 1990; Horton et al., 1990; Langevin et al., 1985; Salter, 1988). All of the informants had been physically, sexually and/or emotionally victimized as children.

Data Collection

In the original study, data collection involved in-depth interviews averaging two hours in length, direct observations during group therapy, and record analysis of 20 incest offenders. Eighteen interviews were tape recorded and transcribed verbatim. Two offenders refused to be tape recorded, and in those cases, extensive notes were taken. Direct observations were made during 65 group therapy sessions and focused on the offenders' behaviors, conversations, and interactions. Record analysis involved an in-depth analysis of the informants' court documents, sexual history, evaluation and test results, treatment assignments, and the charting of individual and group therapy sessions for demographic data and for data that supported or contradicted the themes and patterns that emerged through constant comparative analysis of the interviews and observations. Record analysis also identified variation, filled information gaps, and provided additional details and explanations. Prior to collection of the data, the study proposal was approved by the human subjects committee of the University of Texas at Austin and the facility where the men received treatment. All the men volunteered to be in the study, and a written consent form was signed with the stipulation that a participant could withdraw at any time. Risk to the offenders was considered low as they were already in or had access to treatment, and therapists were available 24 hours a day free of charge if problems surfaced. Confidentiality was maintained at all times by use of a coding system so that the identity of the offenders and responses were known only to the researcher. However, the offenders were reminded prior to the interview that admission of new sexual offenses must, by law, be reported to the law enforcement and social services authorities.

In the expanded study, an additional 22 sex offenders (representing rapists, extrafamilial offenders, exhibitionists, and obscene phone callers) were interviewed; one individually for two hours, the other 21 through a series of focus interviews centering around the fittingness of the remodeling process for other types of sex offenders and variations in remodeling.

- *Figure 1: Remodeling Variations in Adult Male Sex Offenders*

TYPES OF REMODELERS

I. SUCCESSFUL REMODELERS

    A. *COMPREHENSIVE: "I want to change major parts of my life, not just those involved in the abuse."*
    B. *ADEQUATE: "I want to be safe from reoffending."*
        1. *LIMITED: "I'll do my best."*
        2. *GUARDED: "I'll work on just certain areas, others are out of bounds."*
          a. *BUTT OUT: "Some areas are none of your business."*
          b. *TOO ASHAMED: "I'm too ashamed to tell you."*

II. INCOMPLETE REMODELERS

    A. *NOT GET IT: "I just don't get it."*
    B. *DROP OUT: "I'll work hard in treatment, but I'll do what I want outside of treatment."*

III. UNSUCCESSFUL REMODELERS

    A. *IMPOSTOR: "I'll do just enough to look good."*
    B. *DEFIANT: "Nobody can tell me what to do. I'll do what I want."*
    C. *TOTAL DENIER: "I didn't do anything."*
    D. *QUICK FIX: "Just tell me what to do to get out of here."*
    E. *RELAPSER: "I didn't do the upkeep."*

Analysis

Data analysis occurred concurrently with data collection using the constant comparative analysis method (Chenitz and Swanson, 1986; Glaser and Strauss, 1967; Glaser, 1992, 1978; Strauss, 1986; Strauss and Corbin, 1990; Stern, 1980). Following the procedures of constant comparative analysis, once an interview or observation was completed, it was analyzed and coded before going on to the next interview or observation. This allowed the researcher to use the emerging concepts to determine who was to be interviewed next, what questions were to be asked, and what should be observed. As new data were collected, they were analyzed, coded and compared with all the other data before moving on to new sources. Data categories were formed, a core variable was identified

- *Table 1: Sample of Demographic and Remodeling Composite Data on Informants in Grounded Theory Study of Adult Male Incest Offenders Identified by Code*

	Comprehensive	Adequate	Incomplete	Impostor	Resistor
Offenders by category	1, 4, 9, 15, 19	6, 7, 10, 14, 16, 18 limited ability, 13, A, 17 guarded	2, 3 Not get it; 8 dropped out	5, 11, 12	#F, R, T, H
AGE					
< 30	9,15		3		
30-50	1, 19	6, 7, 16, A, 17	5, 8	11, 12	R, T
> 50	4	10, 13, 14, 18	2	F	F, H
ABUSED AS CHILD			8 Denies any; just had "bitter mother"		
Physical	4, 15, 19	6, 7, 13, 14, 17, 18	2, 3	5, 11, 12	
by Mother	1 (Father beat Mother)		3	5	
by Father	4, 9, 15	6, 7 (Some beatings, not too many), 7, 13, 16, 17		5, 11, 12	
Brother		13	2		
Foster brother			3		
Grandfather	4				
Sexual	4, 15, 19	6, 7, 13, 14, 16, A	3	11, 12	F
by Mother	4				
by Father				5, 11, 12	
by Brother		13		12	
by Sister	1 (Sexual with sister, almost same age)				F
by Foster brother			3		
by Grandmother		6			
by Uncle				5	
by Female baby-sitter	15				
by Neighbor boys	1, 4	13, A			12

(remodeling), and an integrated remodeling theoretical framework emerged (Scheela, 1992-a, -b).

Then, using the remodeling framework, all possible demographic and remodeling variables were identified (age, race, IQ, education, occupation, income, marital status, own victimization, response to abuse, family-of-origin relationships, DSM-III-R diagnoses, criminal record, internal and external supports and barriers, type of abuse and type of victims, and response to all the components of the remodeling process) and organized into a table format. Each offender was given a number and his data were placed in the table and compared with each other offender's data. The composite table was 28 pages long (see Table 1 for a sample of the composite table). From this composite table, the types of remodelers were identified and variations noted. The SAT team members involved with offenders, two grounded theory methodology experts, and, most importantly, the offenders themselves validated the analyses.

FINDINGS

The informants indicated the remodeling process was an accurate description of their treatment experience. Based on analysis of the interviews, observations, and chart audits, three main types of remodelers emerged: successful, incomplete, and unsuccessful. Figure 1 lists the types and subtypes discussed below.

Successful Remodelers

The *successful remodelers* work hard in treatment, take responsibility for their abuse and rehabilitation, and successfully graduate from the program. They identify strong interior and exterior supports such as seeking and receiving support from family and/or friends, using support networks to check their own reality, taking responsibility for their abuse and the need for treatment, viewing treatment as an opportunity for help, and working hard in treatment and during the week on treatment tasks. They tend to be honest and open, sometimes even sharing deep dark secrets that no one would have ever known about. Successful remodelers are able to acknowledge and feel feelings, and express remorse and empathy. They demonstrate ego strength and an ability to trust. They exhibit some of the interior and exterior barriers that will be identified with the unsuccessful remodelers, but not to as great an extent or for as long a time.

Successful remodelers tend to do their remodeling in the order of taking on a project, tearing out the damaged parts, rebuilding, and then doing the upkeep. In this way, the changes tend to be internalized and lasting.

The successful remodelers consist of two subtypes, comprehensives and adequates. The *comprehensive remodelers* not only want to prevent reoffending, but also want to make major changes in many other areas of their lives. Their goal is to grow and change. *Adequate remodelers* just want to do enough remodeling to be safe from reoffending. There are two subtypes of inadequates:

❑ *Limited remodelers* who try their best to make changes but are limited by their capabilities and disorders.

❑ *Guarded remodelers* who work on just the areas they choose to change; many areas and problems of their lives are off-limits.

The offenders further subcategorized the guarded remodelers. One type is *butt out*; the offenders decide that some things just are not to be shared in group, "it's none of their business!" Another subcategory of guarded remodelers involves those who are *too ashamed* to share various parts of their abuse and lives. Guilt and shame prevent examination and remodeling of certain areas of their lives.

Incomplete Remodelers

Incomplete remodelers are those offenders who try very hard in the treatment program but just never quite get it or quit before they have completed treatment. The first type, the *not get it* incomplete remodelers, have great difficulty with rebuilding (making the necessary changes) and doing the upkeep (maintaining the changes). Their difficulties are due to lower intellectual abilities and/or psychological or psychiatric disorders. They demonstrate poor judgment when it comes to safe functioning in the community. They do not graduate from treatment. Rather, they remain in a maintenance group indefinitely, where they focus on doing the upkeep (relapse prevention) and receive constant monitoring and guidance. The other subtype of incomplete remodeler, the *drop-out*, does good work while in treatment, however either quits before he has graduated or violates parole or probation and is thus terminated from treatment. For instance, one offender who seemed to be doing good work in treatment violated his probation by secretly seeing his victims. When this was discovered, he was terminated from treatment and sent to prison in another part of the state.

Unsuccessful Remodelers

The *unsuccessful remodelers* fight the treatment program, and if they do not change to a successful or incomplete remodeler, will eventually be terminated from the program. Their interior supports seem to be fewer and operate for shorter periods of time than the successful remodelers. They don't tend to seek support, or if they do, it doesn't feel genuine to the treatment team and the other offenders. There is always the suspicion that behaviors are manipulative, and communication misleading or dishonest. We tend to know the least about these men because they share the least. In contrast to the successful and incomplete remodelers, they are more reticent to take responsibility for abuse and work in treatment. They are less cooperative and do not seem to need answers for why they abused. Their approach is, "Tell me what I need to do to get out of treatment." Treatment is seen as a way to avoid more jail or prison time rather than to grow and change and learn to be safe. The unsuccessful remodelers exhibit many interior and exterior barriers to remodeling. They are much more likely than the successful and incomplete remodelers to continue to deny, minimize and rationalize their abuse, resist treatment tasks, play games, hide information, and break rules. Typically they have a harder time empathizing with their victims, because their focus is on how victimized they are themselves. There are five types of unsuccessful remodelers:

❏ *Impostors* pretend to work hard in treatment, but make few if any real changes. They project an attitude of "I'll do just enough to look good." They know what to say and how to work the system. Imposters are the offenders that slap the paint on or patch leaks rather than engage in any real remodeling. It may be that some of the *guarded adequate* remodelers are really imposters who just get away with their deception.

❏ *Defiants* are uncooperative offenders and do just what they want to do in treatment. Their message is, "Nobody can tell me what to do. I'll do what I want." They do not take on the remodeling process at all, and make their resistance perfectly clear to the treatment team and the other men.

❑ A third type of unsuccessful remodeler, *total deniers*, admit to nothing and insist they are innocent of any crimes. Their typical response when asked to tell their abuse story is, "I didn't do anything." They say there is no need for them to remodel as there is nothing wrong with them.

❑ *Quick fixers,* a fourth type of unsuccessful remodeler, are in a hurry to be out of treatment and have no desire to learn or change. Their attitude is, "Just tell me what I have to do to get out of here as soon as possible." They attempt to rebuild and move on without taking on the responsibility for the abuse and tearing out damaged parts of themselves. The goal is just to look good enough to get out of treatment, not to change.

❑ The last type, *relapsers*, may have successfully graduated from treatment, but didn't maintain the changes and reoffended; they didn't do the upkeep.

These remodeler types are dynamic, thus an offender may begin in one category but progress to others throughout treatment and beyond. For instance, many offenders begin treatment as imposters, defiants, quick fixers, or total deniers, but through treatment, move on to become successful or at least incomplete remodelers. Unfortunately, the movement can also be in the other direction. A few offenders have successfully completed treatment, yet later reoffended. They went from successful guarded remodelers (or perhaps undetected imposters) to unsuccessful relapsers. The SAT program has been in existence since 1983, and the recidivism rate is less than 3%.

CONCLUSIONS AND IMPLICATIONS

The remodeling process and remodeler variations are based on data that emerged from a grounded theory study of 42 adult male incest offenders in one outpatient treatment program, and thus cannot be generalized to other populations. However, the findings of this study suggest the remodeling theoretical framework may be applicable to a broad range of sex offenders (incest offenders, rapists, extrafamilial abusers, exhibitionists, and obscene phone callers). The men indicate the remodeling model is easy for them to understand and relate to as it is in their own words and is a concrete visual metaphor. It serves as a useful tool to orient new offenders to treatment, and to communicate with the men regarding the treatment process and variations. It enables therapists to tailor treatment more specifically to individual offenders. It empha-sizes the need for therapist and treatment flexibility. One therapist put it this way, "We need a whole bag of tricks."

Based on the remodeling framework, the findings indicate sex offend-ers may be successful, incomplete, or unsuccessful remodelers. This treatment typology has numerous treatment implications. One implica-tion is that we can never be totally sure how permanent or real the changes are in an offender or how safe he really is. Research shows that treatment lowers the chances of recidivism (Berner, 1989; Owen and Steele, 1991), but there is no guarantee. On the other hand, the findings support the conclusion that it is never totally hopeless either. An example of this is one offender who graduated from the SAT program in the guarded successful remodeler category. He had satisfactorily completed all the treatment tasks, but the team felt uneasy about his graduating. We couldn't put our finger on it, but his remodeling just didn't seem genuine. Later, he was arrested for reoffending and was sent to prison. I inter-viewed him in prison, and he admitted that he had lied throughout treatment. He had been an imposter in treatment, but had managed to look good enough to graduate. Since being released from prison, he has returned to the treatment program and seems to be functioning at a more genuine level. He would probably now be classified as an adequate if not comprehensive remodeler. Sometimes it seems offenders need to fail several times before they realize "I have a problem and need help."

It is hard to predict outcomes of treatment at this point in time. More research is needed to further develop the remodeler categories and perhaps identify some predictors of treatment success, failure, and recidi-vism. Longitudinal studies, research on other treatment programs and offenders, and studies with larger samples are needed. Future research could also include studies to identify strategies tailored to the various remodeler types, and studies to discover how to move offenders from unsuccessful to successful remodeler categories. The theory of situ-ational leadership (Hersey and Blanchard, 1988) might be a useful model to study in terms of therapist interventions for the various remodeler styles as it posits that leadership styles must vary based on the charac-teristics of those led.

SUMMARY

This study identified successful, incomplete and unsuccessful types of remodelers. Remodeling is a dynamic process; many offenders who start out as unsuccessful remodelers become successful or at least incomplete remodelers and some successful remodelers become unsuccessful remodelers. Treatment implications include the need for flexibility and individualized treatment plans, patience, continual hope of success for offenders, yet healthy skepticism regarding the possibility of recidivism. Much is yet to be learned and continued research in this area is essential.

REFERENCES

Abel, G. G., Becker, J.V., Cunningham-Rathner, J., Mittelman, M., & Rouleau, J. L. (1988). Multiple paraphilic diagnoses among sex offenders. *Bulletin of the American Academy of Psychiatry and the Law,* 16 (2), 153-168.

Ballard, D.T., Blair, G.D., Devereaux, S., Valentine, L.K., Horton, A.L., & Johnson, B. L. (1990). A comparative profile of the incest perpetrator: Background characteristics, abuse history, and use of social skills. In A.L. Horton, B.L. Johnson, L.M. Roundy & D. Williams (Eds.), *The incest perpetrator: A family member no one wants to treat* (Pp. 43-64). Newbury Park, CA: Sage.

Berner, W. (1989).. Voluntary and involuntary treatment of sex offenders. Paper presented at the First International Conference on the Treatment of Sex Offenders, Minneapolis, MN.

Blanchard, G. (1989). *Sex offender treatment: A psychoeducational model.* Golden Valley, MN: Golden Valley Institute for Behavioral Medicine.

Bolton, F., Morris, L.A., & MacEachron, A.E. (1989). *Males at risk: The other side of child sexual abuse.* Newbury Park, CA: Sage.

Carnes, P. (1983). *Out of the shadows: Understanding sexual addiction.* Minneapolis, MN: Compcare.

Chenitz, W.C., Swanson, J.M. (1986). *From practice to grounded theory: Qualitative research in nursing.* Menlo Park, CA: Addison-Wesley.

Christiansen, J. R., & Blake, R. H. (1990). The grooming process in father-daughter incest. In A.L. Horton, B.L. Johnson, L.M. Roundy, & D. Williams (Eds.), *The incest perpetrator: A family member no one wants to treat* (Pp. 88-98). Newbury Park, CA: Sage.

Conte, J. R. (1990). The incest offender: An overview and introduction. In A. L. Horton, B.L. Johnson, L.M. Roundy, & D. Williams (Eds.), *The incest perpetrator: A family member no one wants to treat* (Pp. 19-28). Newbury Park, CA: Sage.

Conte, J.R. (1985). Clinical dimensions of adult sexual abuse of children. *Behavioral Sciences,* 3 (4), 341-354.

Glaser, B.G. (1978). *Advances in the methodology of grounded theory: Theoretical sensitivity.* Mill Valley, CA: Sociology Press.

Glaser, B.G. (1992). *Basics of grounded theory analysis.* Mill Valley, CA: Sociology Press.

Glaser, B.G., & Strauss, A.L. (1967). *The discovery of grounded theory: Strategies for qualitative research.* Chicago: Aldine.

Groth, N., Hobson, W.F., & Gary, T.S. (1982). The child molester: Clinical observations. *Journal of Social Work & Human Sexuality,* 1,129-144.

Hersey, P., & Blanchard, K.H. (1988). *Management of organizational behavior: Utilizing human resources.* Englewood Cliffs, NJ: Prentice-Hall.

Kahn, T.J. (1990). *Pathways: A guided workbook for youth beginning treatment.* Orwell, VT: Safer Society Press.

Knight R.A., & Prentky, R.A. (1990). Classifying sexual offenders: The development and corroboration of taxonomic models. In W.L. Marshall, E.R. Laws, & H.E. Barbaree (Eds.), *The handbook of sexual assault: Issues, theories, and a treatment of the offender.* New York: Plenum.

Langevin, R., Handy, L., Russon, A.E., & Day, D. (1985). Are incestuous fathers pedophilic, aggressive, and alcoholic? In R. Langevin (Ed.), *Erotic preference* (Pp. 161-179). Hillsdale, NJ: Lawrence Erlbaum Associates.

Larson, N.R., & Maddock, J.W. (1986). Structural and functional variables in incest family systems: Implications for assessment and treatment. In T.S. Trepper & M.J. Barrett (Eds.), *Treating incest: A multiple systems perspective.* New York: The Haworth Press, Inc.

Owen, G., & Steele, N.M. (1991). Incest offenders after treatment. In M.Q. Patton (Ed.), *Family sexual abuse: Frontline research and evaluation* (Pp. 178-198). Newbury Park, CA: Sage.

Ryan, G., & Lane, S. (1991). *Juvenile sexual offending: Causes, consequences and corrections.* Lexington, MA: Lexington Books.

Salter, A.C. (1988). *Treating child sex offenders and victims: A practical guide.* Newbury Park, CA: Sage.

Scheela, R.A. (1992-a). The remodeling process: A grounded theory study of adult male incest offenders' perceptions of the treatment process. *Journal of Offender Rehabilitation,* 18 (3/4).

Scheela, R.A. (1992-b). The remodeling process: A grounded theory study of adult male incest offenders' perceptions of the treatment process. In E. Coleman, S.M. Dwyer, and N.J. Pallone (Eds.), *Sex offender treatment: Psychological and medical approaches* (Pp. 167-189). Binghamton, NY: The Haworth Press, Inc.

Scheela, R.A., & Stern, P.N. (In press). Falling apart: A process integral to the remodeling of male incest offenders. *Archives of Psychiatric Nursing.*

Stern, P.N. (1980). Grounded theory methodology: Its uses and processes. *Image,* 12, 20-23.

Strauss, A.L. (1986). *Qualitative analysis for social scientists.* New York: Cambridge University Press.

Strauss, A., & Corbin, J. (1990). *Basics of qualitative research: Grounded theory procedures and techniques.* Newbury Park, CA: Sage.

Trepper, T.S., & Barrett, M.J. (1989). *Systematic treatment of incest: A therapeutic handbook.* New York: Bruner/Mazel.

AUTHOR'S NOTE

Rochelle A. Scheela, Ph.D., R.N., C.S., is professor of nursing at Bemidji State University, a nationally certified clinical specialist in adult psychiatric and mental health nursing, and a therapist in the sexual abuse treatment program at Upper Mississippi Mental Health Center. This research was funded in part by two Minnesota Nurses Association Foundation Research Grants.

Address correspondence to Dr. Rochelle A. Scheela, Bemidji State University, Department of Nursing, Deputy Hall 105, 1500 Birchmont Drive NE, Bemidji, MN 56601.

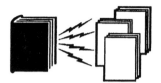

Haworth
DOCUMENT DELIVERY
SERVICE

This valuable service provides a single-article order form for any article from a Haworth journal.

- *Time Saving:* No running around from library to library to find a specific article.
- *Cost Effective:* All costs are kept down to a minimum.
- *Fast Delivery:* Choose from several options, including same-day FAX.
- *No Copyright Hassles:* You will be supplied by the original publisher.
- *Easy Payment:* Choose from several easy payment methods.

Open Accounts Welcome for ...
- Library Interlibrary Loan Departments
- Library Network/Consortia Wishing to Provide Single-Article Services
- Indexing/Abstracting Services with Single Article Provision Services
- Document Provision Brokers and Freelance Information Service Providers

---

MAIL or *FAX* THIS ENTIRE ORDER FORM TO:

Haworth Document Delivery Service
The Haworth Press, Inc.
10 Alice Street
Binghamton, NY 13904-1580

or FAX: 1-800-895-0582
or CALL: 1-800-342-9678
9am-5pm EST

PLEASE SEND ME PHOTOCOPIES OF THE FOLLOWING SINGLE ARTICLES:
1) Journal Title: _____
   Vol/Issue/Year: _____ Starting & Ending Pages: _____
   Article Title: _____
   _____

2) Journal Title: _____
   Vol/Issue/Year: _____ Starting & Ending Pages: _____
   Article Title: _____
   _____

3) Journal Title: _____
   Vol/Issue/Year: _____ Starting & Ending Pages: _____
   Article Title: _____
   _____

4) Journal Title: _____
   Vol/Issue/Year: _____ Starting & Ending Pages: _____
   Article Title: _____
   _____

(See other side for Costs and Payment Information)

COSTS: Please figure your cost to order quality copies of an article.

1. Set-up charge per article: $8.00
($8.00 × number of separate articles) _____

2. Photocopying charge for each article:
1-10 pages: $1.00 _____

11-19 pages: $3.00 _____

20-29 pages: $5.00 _____

30+ pages: $2.00/10 pages _____

3. Flexicover (optional): $2.00/article _____

4. Postage & Handling: US: $1.00 for the first article/
$.50 each additional article _____

Federal Express: $25.00 _____

Outside US: $2.00 for first article/
$.50 each additional article _____

5. Same-day FAX service: $.35 per page _____

GRAND TOTAL: _____

METHOD OF PAYMENT: (please check one)

❏ Check enclosed ❏ Please ship and bill. PO # _____
(sorry we can ship and bill to bookstores only! All others must pre-pay)

❏ Charge to my credit card: ❏ Visa; ❏ MasterCard; ❏ Discover;
❏ American Express;

Account Number: _____ Expiration date: _____

Signature: ✗ _____

Name: _____ Institution: _____

Address: _____

_____

City: _____ State: _____ Zip: _____

Phone Number: _____ FAX Number: _____

MAIL or *FAX* THIS ENTIRE ORDER FORM TO:

Haworth Document Delivery Service
The Haworth Press, Inc.
10 Alice Street
Binghamton, NY 13904-1580

or FAX: 1-800-895-0582
or CALL: 1-800-342-9678
9am-5pm EST)